TEACHING KIDS
TO BUY STOCKS

STORIES AND LESSONS FOR GROWN-UPS

J. J. Wenrich CFP®

Hopeful Hill

PRESS

Teaching Kids to Buy Stocks

Copyright @ 2019 by J.J. Wenrich

First Edition: May 2019

Library of Congress Control Number: 2019903140

ISBN, Hard Cover: 978-1-7337977-0-2

ISBN, Paperback: 978-1-7337977-2-6

ISBN, eBook: 978-1-7337977-1-9

Cover art design: Dave Baldwin and Allyson Cheney

Editing and Interior: Bruce Rowe

Published by Hopeful Hill Press

Hopeful Hill

PRESS

PO Box 73221

San Clemente, California 92673

www.hopefulhillpress.com

Books may be purchased in bulk for education, promotional, and business purposes from your bookseller or by writing to Hopeful Hill Press.

To my friends and family. Thank you for the love and support, even if you had no idea what I was talking about.

To the professionals who shared a conversation with me. Thank you for taking time out of your day.

To Jodie. There are no words. Thank you for loving me.

Contents

Introduction

To many people, the stock market can seem like a mysterious creature, lurking in the shadows of Wall Street. To others, their understanding is at such a brainiac level that they really are speaking a different language than 99 percent of the population. Most of us fall somewhere in between.

If you don't know anything about stocks, this book will help fix that without overwhelming you with nerd words and without making you call yourself a "dummy." I use examples and analogies that anyone can relate to.

Maybe you know a thing or two about the market—you have mutual funds and a 401(k)—but are unsure about buying individual stocks. This book will help you become more comfortable with pulling the "buy trigger" on your first stock.

No matter your understanding, this book will help educate you about the stock market as well as entertain you along the way. I will tell you the same stories I've told to both kids and professionals—as well as professionals who act like kids—over my 20-year career in the investment business.

If the stock market seems too big and complex to you, then follow along as I show you how I taught the basics to my kids. Over the course of several years, I was able to help them understand the fundamentals of long-term, buy-and-hold investing in individual stocks.

I'll walk you through how I encouraged my three kids to save their birthday and allowance money over the course of several years, then use a portion of that money to buy stocks. You'll learn the lessons I've tried to teach both my kids, and thousands of financial professionals over the past 20 years. No matter where you are in your investing life, I think you'll find this book enjoyable and entertaining.

The basics are, well...basic

In my opinion, the basics of investing are not terribly complicated. Don't get me wrong, it can become complicated very quickly. "Investment people" love to make things sound more complex than they really are.

They love to make a new word for things that already have words. Words like "hedge" and "long" and "short" and it will have nothing do with bushes or length. It can seem incomprehensible to outsiders, while to insiders, they don't realize they're speaking another language.

In my career, I've found myself giving hundreds of speeches on "what's going on in the stock market" to folks who don't speak the language. I've found myself being the information conduit between brainiac investor nerds and regular, everyday people. A large part of my career has also involved teaching financial professionals; in essence, teaching them the language.

Along the way, I've also taught my three kids how to buy their first stocks. First, I taught them to save their cash into a savings account. Then, while they were saving cash, I taught them the principles of investing in stocks. I use the same teaching process with adults. I will guide you through that process in this book.

I've been able to do this by simplifying the concepts to a level that even a kid can understand. I began talking to my children about investing and buying stocks when they were ages three, four, and five. I was able to teach them things in slow steps, as part of our everyday conversations.

I was amazed at how well they could understand basic concepts of business and investing. At such a young age, they aren't clouded by bias and have no lessons to unlearn. The things my kids said blew my mind. I found myself quoting those most profound statements at presentations in front of hundreds of people.

For me, it is surreal sitting on a stage in front of 200 investors, next to a portfolio manager who manages a $5 billion fund, quoting your 10-year-old son about what dividends mean to a long-term investor.

I've also learned a great deal by asking fellow investment professionals about their conversations with their children. I've had the luxury of being able to casually interview moms and dads while we talk about the markets. I typically ask anyone who has kids, "Do you talk to your kids about stocks?" I get some great answers, and it helps spark a conversation.

In the course of my job working with investment and financial planning professionals, I've also shared my successes in teaching my kids to buy stocks. I've seen some professionals I meet become inspired by my story and begin to teach their kids. In fact, one of those conversations led me to write this book.

Now, let's get going. Read on and you will find the lessons I've taught my kids, as well as some of the best lessons I've heard from others.

1 | A Little About Me and My Family

I grew up in a town of about 100 people outside Wichita, Kansas. Although the "big city" of Wichita was nearby, I was far removed from Wall Street in my rural town.

At home, we really didn't discuss the stock market. My dad talked once or twice about a couple of stocks he said he owned, and my mom said she had some retirement accounts, but that was the extent of it. My mom did help me open a checking account in sixth grade, and even taught me how to reconcile it.

I was fortunate to go to great public schools where we were taught several aspects of business and personal finance. I am so thankful that I had such progressive and engaged teachers in the small towns that made up our rural community.

Out of necessity...

Out in the country, we didn't have cable. We had four channels, one of which was PBS. In Kansas, it's cold in the winter, it rains all spring, and it's 100 degrees and humid all summer. I was inside watching TV more than I should have been and I watched the news a lot as a kid. From 5:00 to 6:30 p.m. there was NOTHING ON except for news.

From all that news watching, I became very curious about the stock market, and fascinated by *how many* stocks there were.

Now's a good time for a first lesson to help you understand the following paragraph.

Nerd Word Alert

Stock (Ticker) Symbol: An abbreviation used to identify shares of a particular company traded on a stock market. "Ticker" is a remnant of a time when stock quotes were transmitted using a dedicated stock ticker machine that typed out prices on a moving paper tape.

Each company stock has its own set of letters that act as a symbol or code

5

to represent it, similar to how an element on the periodic table has its own symbol. Some are logical, some are not. For example, the symbol for Apple is AAPL. Makes sense, right? The AT&T ticker symbol is T. That's a little tougher. Southwest Airline's ticker symbol is LUV—you need to know a little about the company to understand that one.

I was always amazed that there were people who could just name symbol after symbol like it was nothing. All these years later...I'm one of those people.

Before computers, you would read the stock quotes in the newspaper and they were listed alphabetically by ticker symbol. If you didn't know that T meant AT&T, it could be difficult to find your stock. Today you can just ask Siri or Alexa.

Thanks Mrs. Brown

Maybe one of the most important days of my childhood came in seventh grade. At the time, Kansas State University sponsored a stock market game for junior high and high school students. In this game, you were given a make-believe $100,000 to invest as you saw fit.

This was a few years before the internet, so you had to physically mail your trades to K-State each day. You would write in the ticker symbol and number of shares to buy or sell and fill in bubbles with a No. 2 pencil. Your buying or selling price for the stock would be the price at the market open of the date following the postmark on the envelope you mailed. K-State mailed rankings to the schools weekly.

My seventh-grade teacher, Mrs. Brown, enrolled us in that game, and invited a stockbroker from "the city" (Wichita) to speak to us. I remember him talking about things like: What is a stock? What is a bond? What is the Dow?

The U.S. was in recession that year, and I remember him handing us an article from The Wall Street Journal titled "Recession-Proof Stocks." The only stock I remember from that article is Waste Management, but that makes sense. You still throw stuff away no matter what the state of the economy.

I was completely enamored by what he told us; I was hooked. I called my mom when I got home and asked her to bring home graph paper, so I could start to chart prices of stocks from the newspaper.

Back in the late '80s it wasn't as easy to get information. We didn't have the internet, so I relied on the daily newspaper and my four television stations. I needed the graph paper to make a chart. I didn't have much disposable income in seventh grade—and I wasn't giving up Sports Illustrated to get The Wall Street Journal—so I drew my own charts.

After a few weeks in the contest, our team was second in the state, mostly on the back of Dow Chemical, the stock that the broker helped us pick the day he visited. Then I made a classic investing mistake.

My mom was a nurse and worked for a family doctor nicknamed "Dr. D." When she told Dr. D that I was interested in stocks, he told her, "He should check out Michaels Stores" because that's what he was buying. I went to Mrs. Brown and told her what I heard. She walked me to the principal's office (a walk I knew well) to use his phone to ask the opinion of the broker who came to our class. I don't remember much of what he said that day other than "they have a continuous problem with inventory."

After we picked up Michael's Stores thanks to Dr. D, we saw our ranking quickly drop out of the top 10. When I didn't listen to the broker and instead listened to the doctor with a "hot tip," I lost our fake money.

There's a lesson there—don't trust the guy with the hot stock pick! Do your own research and find people you can trust and that know your situation. When in doubt, go with the professional.

We played the same stock market game one year in high school as well. I can't say I was as passionate about stocks then as I was in seventh grade (and later in college), but those great teachers out in the country taught me the accounting, math, writing, and social psychology skills that still carry me. One thing you will learn when you start buying stocks; the psychology skills are just as important as the math skills.

My freshman year at The University of Kansas, my roommate's Dad was a self-taught commodities trader, and made a good living selling a newsletter on the topic, as well as trading his own money from home full time. My roommate had always talked about doing the same and that seemed interesting. I liked that he was self-taught. I also liked that he was his own boss and could just watch the markets all day.

Finally, in my senior year, I had a professor who truly loved the stock market. Those experiences reignited that same flame I had found in junior high.

Here's how hot that flame burned. During spring break my senior year, while all my buddies drove down to Mexico to party, I stayed in Lawrence and geeked out on stock charts, spreadsheets, and CNBC. I remember trying to stay up all night to watch the Asian and European markets. I would wake up, look at the markets for a few minutes, then go back to sleep. I slept on the floor in front of the TV in the living room all week like this. It was epic.

Since then, there aren't too many days that go by that I'm not following the market. Unless I'm forcing myself to ignore it or off the grid, I'm tuned in.

Two decades in investments and financial planning

My first six years out of college, from 2000 to 2006, I opened my own financial planning practice for families and individuals as part of a franchise with a major broker-dealer.

During my first year of being a financial planner and building my practice from the ground up, I married a fellow financial planner who had started about the same time as me. Jodie was six years older than me and had sole-custody of her 10-year-old son Alexx. When we married, we combined our practices and eventually opened our own, independent office.

Jodie and I worked together, helping families build long-term financial plans. We helped them develop comprehensive financial plans.

A comprehensive plan includes strategies to save cash, invest for retirement and college goals, reduce taxes, cover risks (insurance), and make sure end-of-life affairs are in order (wills, trusts, and estate planning).

The appendix of this book includes a "Quick and Simple Financial Planning Checklist" for you to use as a personal guide for yourself.

I also recommended reading a book just published by a friend of mine: "The Balancing Act" by Dave Baldwin[2].

Even when we know what we *should* do to create a healthy financial life, it's hard to do. His book helps us learn *why* we make the choices we make, and how to combat those natural biases toward living beyond our means. Rather than "cutting back," the result can be contentment and achieving the goals that are most important to you.

The family grows

In October 2006, having recently had our second child in 16 months, Jodie and I no longer wanted to run the business. I wanted to work with professional investors, and Jodie wanted to be a full-time mom. We made the decision to sell our business and see what the future would bring. Before the end of the year I went to work for a global investment company based in Kansas City. My clients were some of the best investment professionals and financial advisors in the western U.S.

Then by the end of 2007, we had our third child in 30 months. Here we were, with three children under three and a teenager!

I give you that background, because this little family unit is the basis for the lessons I am teaching. You and your spouse don't have to be financial planners to teach your kids healthy financial habits or to teach them to buy stocks, but it has certainly helped me write this book for you.

In my career, I've traveled millions of miles and presented to thousands of financial professionals as well as "individual savers" who don't know much about the market. "Not knowing" didn't keep these savers from being successful.

You don't need to be brilliant, you just need to be disciplined to be a good stock investor. You need to follow some guidelines, which I will cover, and exercise patience and prudence. You also need to be wary of greed in yourself and others, and understand that every investor will lose money at some point. *That* is the only guarantee in investing.

Note

1) *The Balancing Act*, Dave Baldwin, 2019, www.thebalancingactbook.com

2 | The $500 Challenge: A Bait and Switch

It all started with a silly bet I made with my kids when they were roughly ages three, four, and five. That's Max, Henry, and Annabel—oldest to youngest.

Once a child realizes that money can be traded for "stuff," they seem to have a natural tendency to want to make that trade happen as soon as possible.

"These coins and bills are fun and all dad, but can we go get some toys and candy now? I mean right now—as much as I can get."

I watched them immediately spend everything they ever received.

At the time, the five of us were living in a small apartment just so we could save money. I wanted to teach our kids the lesson that you should sacrifice to save, rather than spend, spend, spend. For motivation, I told the kids, "If you save $500, I'll match it."

I knew it would take at least two to three years to save $500 dollars unless they found a way to earn extra money. Their only real source of income was from birthday and holiday gifts.

I also wanted to see them trying to find ways to earn extra money beyond waiting for gifts twice a year. It was about that time we started to pay allowance for chores. When I needed some extra help for other miscellaneous chores, I was also known to pay extra. If they weren't being particularly helpful in a given week, we would remind them of the $500 challenge and sometimes it helped.

Over time, we found they cared more about chores because of the goal. More importantly, they cared more about saving their money. We opened a savings account for each of them at the bank, and they began to deposit their money.

Anyone with siblings knows almost anything can turn into a competition. With three kids within 30 months of each other in age, almost *everything* turns into a competition. Saving money was no different. The perpetual one-upping took over and all three saved their money fairly aggressively to hit the $500 goal.

When I announced the competition, I did it without consulting my wife. Note to all you dads out there: you should probably talk to your wife first.

She heard me tell the kids, "If you save $500, I'll give you $500. You'll have $1,000. How rad is that?" Though she liked the idea of incenting them to save, she wondered if we were creating a problem if they succeeded.

What she didn't hear me tell them, is that they would not just have $1,000 to blow on whatever. This $1,000 would be their financial foundation for when they were older. They didn't necessarily have to save it until then, but I reminded them that you never know when something will come up where you'll need money.

At age four or five, you don't know what's in front of you yet. Maybe you'll really be into sports and need the money for a special camp. Maybe you'll be into music and want an expensive instrument. Maybe you'll be into science and want a particular telescope, or into engineering and use it to build a robot that smashes other robots!

Maybe you don't spend it on anything like that and you want a car when you're old enough. Maybe you use it to buy a diamond ring for your future wife. (Boys: "Yuck. Gross. No way, dad!" Annabel: <Swoon>)

Maybe you keep it for an emergency fund when you're an adult or in college. (All: Yeah...that sounds *great*, dad.) Bad example, even if it's practical.

What I *didn't* tell the kids—and what I *did* tell Jodie when she questioned my sanity on this idea—is that I would match the money into a stock account at Scottrade. They would have to pick their own stock or stocks with the $500 we gave them. They would then have $500 in savings at the bank, and $500 invested.

My bonus at the company where I worked was in company stock—and the 401(k) match was in the investments in the 401(k)—so why not make their match in stock as well?

I'm not saying that this was my plan or idea going into the conversation with the kids. I was likely completely winging it when this all started.

If I recall correctly, I came up with the stock idea when Jodie didn't look convinced that young kids would understand that they couldn't spend the money we just gave them. She may have been convinced, but sometimes I read her face instead of reading her mind, and this was one of those occasions. Her face was saying "you're nuts!" even if she never said it.

To further sell the idea (since I had already promised the kids), I came up with the stock idea on the spot.

"Besides, I'm not giving them cash. I'm going to match it into a Scottrade account. If we match it with stock, it will give them the next couple years while they're saving to start learning about stocks and the stock market. By then, they can have an idea of what they might want to buy."

Wow, that actually *sounded* really good and is a great idea. (Nice work panic button!)

Jodie: "Did you tell the kids that's what we're doing?"

Me: "No but I will eventually..."

Silence.

Eventually I told them what was really up and that it would be for their own good, blah blah blah. Whatever, it was a bait and switch...and I'm ok with it. I explained that it's important to have a cash cushion—at their ages $500 should be sufficient—and then invest the rest.

I also reminded them that the money might grow if they invest it and that they might want that money some day for a car (assuming your mom and dad think you are responsible enough—clears throat aggressively) or college or to move out of your mom and dad's house or something. (Since that's what they were probably thinking once they realized they had been baited and switched.)

As I write this, they have not touched the $500 they saved. It is still in a savings account at the bank. The $500 we matched has been invested and have each added to their investments when coaxed to do so.

To start, Henry bought four shares of Apple for $110. Annabel bought four shares of Disney at $90. Max split the difference and bought two of each. When Henry bought Apple, he said, "If it reaches $200, I'll sell half." He carried through on that, but actually sold at $210.

It has been a great learning tool in many ways. It helped them learn to save, not spend. It helped them learn to keep a cash cushion. And it helped them learn some very valuable lessons about both the math and the psychology of investing.

It didn't solve that tendency to want to spend everything they have, but they still save more than they did before the contest.

3 | The Annual Stock Market Game

When we moved to California from Kansas, we began homeschooling our kids, but did it by hiring a teacher to come to our home. Seeing how instrumental my seventh-grade stock market game was in my life, I wanted to incorporate it into our homeschool curriculum. One evening, in similar fashion to how the $500 Savings Challenge started, the Annual Stock Market Game began.

Each year on the Tuesday after Labor Day, the contest begins and then runs through the Friday before the next year's Labor Day. Why do we run it this way? To coincide with the beginning of the school calendar year (smart answer) and I probably came up with the idea on Labor Day weekend (correct answer).

The kids each choose two stocks to hold from the beginning to the end of the contest period with no changes allowed once it begins. We simulate a portfolio of 50 percent in each stock. The portfolio that has the highest return after the 12-month period is the winner.

I have a small trophy made for the winner that includes the two stocks they selected and the rate of return for the hypothetical portfolio.

Even as our school situation has evolved, we've continued with the contest for our three youngest children. Every Labor Day weekend, we settle the returns from the previous year's contest and pick the stocks for next year.

I've not been participating in the contest. I mean, that wouldn't be fair, right? I'm a professional! (Sarcasm intended).

I'm not sure how I escaped the scrutiny of participation in this game. Perhaps because it started as part of the homeschool setup, I was able to avoid the humiliation of likely being beaten by one (or all) of my kids. However, it looks like beginning in 2018-2019, mom and dad will be participating in the contest as well, though the trophy will still go to the winner of the contest between the three youngest kids. The bragging rights on those trophies are far too powerful a force to dare disrupt.

Contest results

2014 – 2015:

- Annabel +20.0% – Rite Aid (RAD) and Disney (DIS)
- Henry +11.3% – PetSmart (PETM)* and Apple (AAPL)
- Max - 4.9% – Southwest Air (LUV) and Ford (F)

PETM was taken private during the contest and the proceeds stayed in cash.

2015 – 2016:

- Max +4.9% – Microsoft (MSFT) and Target (TGT)
- Henry +0.9% – Best Buy (BBY) and Target (TGT)
- Annabel -5.8% – Disney (DIS) and Netflix (NFLX)

2016 – 2017:

- Annabel +42.2% –Disney (DIS) and Netflix (NFLX)
- Max +35.5% – Nintendo (NTDOY) and Google (GOOG)
- Henry +25.8% – Microsoft (MSFT) and Google (GOOG)

Annabel showing off both of her trophies. Annabel went from worst to first in 2016-17. She kept the same portfolio from 2015-16 and it proved successful.

2017 – 2018:

- Max +73.5% –Amazon (AMZN) and Apple (AAPL)
- Annabel +57.3% – Netflix (NFLX) and Facebook (FB)
- Henry +21.6% –Apple (AAPL) and Facebook (FB)

Max (13) and his trophy from 2017-2018.

4 | Welcome to the "Shark Tank"

If you do nothing else, I recommend, watch the CNBC show "Shark Tank" with your kids. You will be doing a decent chunk of the work in this book without realizing it. Not only is the show highly entertaining, it is real life investing and all that goes along with it. It helps kids begin to speak the language of business.

This show has been instrumental in teaching my kids to think like a stock picker. The stock picking process includes evaluating the story, numbers, and expectations for a business. Watching "Shark Tank" naturally leads you down this path of thinking.

When you watch "Shark Tank," you're watching small and typically young companies (usually a one- or two-person operation) asking for new investors to join their business.

Watch the show with your kids and actively talk about the businesses being pitched to the Sharks. Ask each other questions like this:

- What is the product?
- Would you buy it?
- How easy would it be for competitors to do the same thing?
- What do you like or not like about the product?
- What do you think about the offer prices and asking prices?
- Would you buy into the business if you were a Shark?
- Was it a good or bad deal for the business? Remember, sometimes a good idea can be a bad deal.

Pay particular attention to the company's pricing of the offers. Based on the price and percentage of the company they are willing to part with for that price, you can figure out what they believe the company is worth. If the company says they're asking for $100,000 for 50 percent of the company, they think the total company is worth $200,000. If they say they want $100,000 for 25 percent of the company, then they think the company is worth $400,000.

You will usually also hear the Sharks dig into the numbers a little deeper and ask, "How many are you selling per year?" or "How much profit are you making per year?"

The question all of the sharks are asking themselves is, "How long will it take me to get paid back?" You'll find in the stock picking process, investors think about stocks the same way.

Among the Sharks, Kevin O'Leary (aka Mr. Wonderful) is often a good one to watch for this. At some point he always seems to boil it down to the bottom line, saying "I want to know how this is going to make me money."

That's an important thing to think about in a business. Who wants to go into business to lose money? Not me! Good business people and investors think to themselves "How long will it take me to get paid back and start making money?"

The "Shark Tank" teaches this lesson, and so many others, very well. You even see a fair amount of kids on the show, proving that there are plenty of kids doing extraordinary things in business.

5 | Talk To Your Kids About Money

This may seem obvious, but...talk to your kids about money. Talk to them about how much things cost so they have a sense of scale. I'm not suggesting you tell them how much money you make (unless you want *everyone* to know), but let them know how much things in their world cost.

Start to have this conversation about money and cost just as you do when you teach them the rest of the foundations of life; the same way we teach them to look both ways when crossing the street and to wash their hands. Teach it to them as it happens while you are together, and find a way to make it relative to their world too.

When I was four years old, there was a general store across from my local church. On Sunday after church we would sometimes go to that store to get pop or candy. I remember one day taking a pocket full of change into the store and putting two candy bars on the counter and the clerk saying, "That'll be 60 cents, son." I threw a handful of change on the counter, and he said, "You need a little more, son." I threw a few more coins on the counter, and he gave me some of them back. It was then I realized, "Some of these coins are worth more than others and if I want to buy anything good, I better have 30 cents because that's what a candy bar costs." I will forever in my mind have a baseline of 60 cents for two candy bars because of the general store.

If your child's world is a toy or treat, then tell them the cost in dollars. If their world is Pokémon cards, then make sure they know how much a pack of Pokémon cards costs. Whatever they are into, make sure they understand the dollar value, even if they don't yet understand what a dollar is worth. It will give them a baseline for the future as they learn about the cost of things.

A friend told me a story about her teenage son and his spending habit on snacks and food. He would use his iPhone to pay for stuff at school or when he was out and about. Two dollars here, $4 there. The family used software that tracked the family spending, and also for each individual. He was pretty shocked to find out he had spent $1,500 of his own money on "snacks" over the course of the year. His reply, "That's a drone's worth of snacks!"

One day my kids were watching me fill my truck with gas, and they saw it was over $80 to fill the tank. They were blown away. In fact, my oldest (12 at the time) told his brother and sister, "That's not *really* $80 to fill the tank; we're reading it wrong or something." My wife quickly replied, "It most certainly is correct and maybe we need to do a better job of talking about how much life costs."

How will kids know if we don't teach them?

Also teach them to be value conscious and that the same thing might have a different price depending on where you buy it. If you observe a big markup on something, where the company is undoubtedly making a lot of profit, point it out to them. Doing these things will not only help them be more prudent consumers as they grow up, it will help them recognize good businesses and therefore, good investment opportunities.

A teaching example for me is the "endcap" at a retailer. An endcap is a display of products at the end of a store aisle. When I shop with my kids, I'm a little nutty about never buying off an endcap. Having worked in retail and with a good University of Kansas business school education, I learned that these items are not always the best deal in town. Maybe they are, maybe not. But I always make sure I'm not missing a competitive product to those on the endcap or a better deal in some other way.

The endcap makes me suspicious because I know it's a game of psychology for marketers. I can't help but tell my poor kids these things when we shop together. (Maybe *that's* why I shop alone so much as they get older.)

Chores and allowance

I am a believer in allowance, and I am a believer in chores. Not every chore should be paid an allowance but paying for a few can help teach kids important lessons.

Helping out also helps kids develop a sense of pride and independence. Find a balance between rewarding some activities with money and teaching them that some activities are just part of being on the team. As a parent, you'll find the right balance for your family.

What's the right amount to pay kids for allowance? I don't profess to have the right answer to this question. It depends on many factors, including age, household economics, etc.

I've heard some great stories about how other parents deal with how much to pay. One of my favorites I heard secondhand, so I cannot attest to its accuracy, but it's a good enough story that I'll share it anyway. (Besides, don't let accuracy ruin a good story!)

There was a particular, top-performing financial professional who made his kids negotiate with him each week for their allowance. Allegedly, to kick off the session he would ask them, "What do you think you deserve this week?" Maybe they would throw a ridiculous amount out there and he would say yes or no, but it would get things started and they would come to terms from there.

I can say I tried it a few times, and the results were—at the very least—interesting. Two of my kids were particularly quick to learn, and another was so annoyed by the process he just kind of gave up and said, "I don't care. Just pay me, or don't, but please don't make me go through this."

We all know our kids pretty well, and sometimes it's good to find out they are bad at something to prevent putting them at a disadvantage. I found out two of my three kids are really good at negotiating. I also found that they may need to accompany their older brother when he makes a big purchase to prevent him from getting fleeced. We all have our skills, and sometimes it's good to know what we don't know.

Teaching with chores

No matter how busy we all are, a chore here or there stacked into the rhythm of the day can help make everyone's life better and teaches kids a great life lesson. While you're waiting on your toast, run the recycling out or empty the dishwasher. On your way upstairs to change and shower, feed the fish...and don't forget to make your bed.

From an early age, you can teach kids to pick up their toys, do little things to help you (or at least pretend to help you), and develop a sense of pride for doing it. Most adults will need to clean up after themselves and do their own laundry at some point in their lives, so you might as well teach your kids along the way. It also helps kids build self-esteem to be able to contribute to the household duties. Thank them and let them know, "I couldn't do it without your help!"

Now to a busy mom or dad, this isn't the easy way out most times. You can probably get it done quicker by doing it yourself but find that balance between just getting it done and investing the time in your child so they can do it for themselves.

For most of our kids' school years we've used a "chore chart" for various daily and weekly chores. Each morning, the kids do their chores before school as part of their daily routine. It has become so routine that they almost sleepwalk through it the way I sleepwalk through my morning stock charts. (The stock market opens at 6:30 a.m. on the West Coast).

We found the app BusyKid to be a fantastic resource for our kids when we began using it in 2018. It can be either a replacement or a complement to the chore chart. The kids enjoy using it to check off their chores on their iPads to earn their allowance each week. You can also set BusyKid up so allowance is paid to a debit card for them, with funds electronically transferred from your bank account upon your approval. This has actually proven to be our kids "checking account," complete with a debit card.

Over time, you can use some of these chores as a means to teach them the value of money in combination with paying an allowance. You cannot teach kids how to manage or invest money if they don't have any. I don't know that just giving money to them teaches them to value it either. Most of us work for our money, and most likely most of our kids will have to work for their money when they are adults.

Allowance also provides another way to teach kids some level of scale for how much things cost. Teaching kids that you have to work X amount to pay for Y is important for them to appreciate the value of a dollar, just like teaching them that some things are worth doing for no money. It's all about that balance, and chores and allowance help teach both.

There's also the question of paying for school grades. I see no problem with it. I still think kids should do chores, but I also understand how busy things get. If your kids are excelling at school and activities and don't have time for chores, that's OK. Find a reward system.

Maybe you do a few things; that's what we do. Allowance for chores tends to be weekly while pay for grades tends to be by school period (semi-semester or semester). Plus, I've been known to pay bonuses for remarkably rad tricks at the skatepark.

We lead busy lives, and our kids lead busier lives than many of us ever did. Activities are stacked from morning to night, and time at home can be precious. I also know that despite all this, moms and dads across the globe keep just as busy a schedule as their kids do and make it all work.

It's important to find the little things in the course of the day that make the household flow with a little better rhythm. If we can reward those little behaviors to help us teach kids both "life rhythm" as well as the value of a dollar, that's a win-win and might buy mom and dad a little sanity at the end of a long day.

TCB

I've taught my kids that their school work, activities, and chores are their "business." It's their responsibility to take care of their business. This started with Jodie and me raising Alexx through his teenage years. We began telling him to TCB—take care of your business—so you can get more freedom and trust from mom and dad.

This funny little family saying evolved from watching the TV sitcom Seinfeld when we first were married. There is an episode where Kramer finds himself in the corporate world by happenstance. When Jerry asks him what he does all day, he answers coyly, "TCB—takin' care of business." This always made me laugh and I ended up stealing the line to help teach Alexx, and eventually the three "littles," that work is part of life, but it's worth doing it so you can enjoy a better life.

As our little ones grew up, we continue to teach them this about their chores and schoolwork. I will tell them, "Hey—TCB! Take care of your business before you take care of your play."

TCB applies to all of us as we go through our busy times. I've been on the road a lot in my career, and that puts pressure on Jodie and the kids. We would get through it by saying, "TCB—taking care of business." And we'll make up for it with quality time on the other side of the sacrifices.

Now, the hippest readers are already thinking about Elvis Presley. I was informed that TCB was also on the tail of Elvis's private jet, and it too stood for taking care of business. I don't know if he meant it the same way as I do and won't speculate, but if it's good enough for Kramer and Elvis, how could I go wrong?

If you want a different twist on this idea, we're also known to tell our kids "Think Bee! Think Bee!" from Jerry Seinfeld's The Bee Movie.

I grind, you grind

School, chores, allowance? Yes. Lather, rinse, repeat. It is a grind, but that's OK. Life is about learning to find balance within that grind. I had a boss who said, "You grind for me; I'll grind for you." In fact, he said that to us in the context of how he told his (at the time) 12-year-old daughter to handle *her* business. He told her "I'm grinding for you every day. All I ask is that you grind for me too and we'll meet together throughout the week."

Combine all these lessons into one, and give your kids a list of chores each day and/or week, then pay them an allowance to help them learn to have money and manage it. I think it correlates perfectly to the real world. Whether you're running your own business or working for someone, you work—you get money.

If you don't like working for a living, save your money and make it work for you. If you save enough money and invest it wisely, eventually you can let it do some or all the working for you. Money doesn't grow on trees, but as I will show you, you can plant a money tree for yourself by knowing a few simple things.

Help kids find the entrepreneur within

Kids have great imaginations. If left alone in a room with nothing, they will come up with new games on their own. If you teach them about money, you'll be surprised how quickly they become entrepreneurial.

I've watched my kids try to develop different businesses with various levels of success. My daughter (and youngest) used her earnings to build a baking business with a friend. Both homeschooled, they decided to use their flexible schedule to bake cupcakes between the end of their lessons and the end of public school. They then set up shop on the sidewalk between the neighborhood and the school and sold them to the public-school kids on their way home.

Not to be outdone, our middle son found a better way. He biked to Target, bought a bulk pack of Smarties and Snickers bars, and sold them individually on the same sidewalk. Why put all that work into cupcakes when you can make a bigger margin on someone else's work?

Later, the scene at dinner was similar to any mafia-head *famiglia* meeting ever held. There was discussion of who owned what territory on what days.

In the end they never reached much of a conclusion because none of them really wanted to work every day anyhow. After a few days, the work started to feel like work, plus they ended up eating most of their profits.

What's the point in telling this story? Giving the kids a financial base gave them the understanding of money to help them think about how a business works and how to use that knowledge to build something bigger with those resources.

Encourage your kids to be entrepreneurial. It helps them begin to incorporate the concept into their daily activities, whether it be playing make-believe or actually trying to start their own little business. It helps them begin to speak the language.

Share. Save. Spend.

We also tried to always teach our kids: "Share. Save. Spend." Preferably in that order.

- Share: Even when we were broke-as-a-joke, we shared what we really didn't have to share. When you do that, it comes back to you. We truly believe this.
- Save: Set something aside for a rainy day before you decide how you are going to spend it. As financial planners say, "Pay yourself first." Put money in savings before you pay the bills.
- Spend: Once you've done these things, you can prioritize how you will spend it, and the time you take to share and save first may keep that money from burning a hole in your pocket.

The BusyKid app I mentioned before even uses a similar "Save–Share–Spend" philosophy, allowing you to both donate to charity and invest in stocks within the app.

Business is happening all around you

Begin to have conversations with your kids about businesses you see every day. Chances are, most of the time you're spending money there's a business associated with it. Help your kids be aware that there are businesses all around that you take for granted. Some are small, locally-run operations. Some are enormous corporations that could become potential stock picks for them.

Talk about how a particular company makes money if you know. It doesn't have to be complicated. If you're at a restaurant, explain how the business tries to make a profit by spending less on food, staff, and rent than it receives from customers buying food.

If you're at the grocery store, explain how the grocery store buys things in bulk at "wholesale" prices and sells it to us for more. We pay more because of the service the store provides: the convenience of a huge selection of products in one location. Explain that the products the grocery store or restaurant sells also represent other businesses for other companies If you are buying veggies or milk, there's a farmer out there working hard to make that happen. If they are paying rent, there's a landlord that owns the building as a business.

As you talk about the businesses you see around you, start talking about the difference between public and private companies. Wait a minute—public and private companies—that sounds a little like nerd words. These were my kids' first investment nerd words; maybe they'll be your first too. Here's a quick explanation.

Nerd Word Alerts

Privately owned: Businesses that are not available to buy or sell in the stock market. With private ownership, there is no formal exchange or marketplace, so it may take days or months or years to find a buyer or seller.

Publicly traded: Businesses that are available to own in the stock market. A private business becomes public by offering shares to the public in an "initial public offering" or IPO.

As a company grows, it may find it needs more investment money to grow faster. There are various ways a company can get more money to grow. They can borrow from a bank or from investors, but that money has to be paid back and also has a cost associated with it. They can also ask for new investors to join the business, and instead of having to pay the money back, they offer a share of profits in return, just like on Shark Tank.

Once our kids started thinking about this, they would routinely ask, "Is so-and-so company publicly-traded?" If I didn't know the answer, we would do some "Googling" together to find out.

In those early years, the most frequent question was, "Is Lego publicly traded?" The answer we found was no, it's not. It's a privately-owned company called The Lego® Group based in Billund, Denmark. The company is still owned by the Kirk Kristiansen family who founded it in 1932. (Note that this is the Legobricks side of the business. The theme parks are owned by a separate company.)

The point of all of this is to encourage you to talk to your kids about money as early as you can. Encourage them to participate in the household work to earn their money. Teach them the value of money early and often. It helps them learn the language of business, and provides a foundation for future lessons, including how to buy stocks when they are ready.

If we're preparing our kids for the real world, we owe it to them to teach them how to handle and understand money. I used the conversation about money to springboard my kids towards even larger lessons about stocks. Using simple, commonsense analogies we can teach them to turn savings into assets, and assets into a financial base to build a future upon.

6 | The Most Powerful Force

> "Compound interest is the most powerful force in the universe."—Albert Einstein

Nerd Word Alerts

Interest: Money paid or received as compensation for depositing or loaning money.

Compound Interest: Earning interest on interest, over time.

Rate of Return: The money earned on an investment expressed as a percentage of the original investment. Investing $100 and earning $10 is a rate of return of: $10 ÷ $100 = 0.10 = 10%

What exactly is compound interest? Without making things more complicated than they need to be, Einstein is referring to what happens to a sum of money that earns a return, then is left alone to keep earning a return on that return, again and again over time. "Over time" takes patience. Patience pays though. As you will see, interest on interest can turn into a lot of money.

Let me show you a few examples the same way I showed my kids one afternoon. Like many my age who grew up before Microsoft Excel was mainstream, I learned about compounding on a calculator. An HP-10B to be exact. Excel is *much* better.

You can do the year by year calculations below on a regular calculator as we go. See the Appendix for the Excel commands used in the examples, so you can show your kids (or yourself).

If you don't feel like going to Excel, just follow the tables below and concentrate on the beginning and ending numbers. When looking at the tables, place a notecard or bookmark below the line you are reading to help focus your eyes on only that line.

Getting started

One afternoon, I said to the kids, "You saved $500, and I'm matching you $500. You have $1,000. I'm going to show you how to turn that $1,000 into $2,000 or more by the time you graduate college in 10 to 15 years."

You have options for how you can save this money. Each option will give you a different "rate of return." You can keep it in cash and put it in your piggy bank for the next 10 years. In 10 years, you will have $1,000. While that may seem like the "safe" choice, most things like food and a place to live cost more over time. That $1,000 won't pay for as much in 10 years as it does now. (More on that later in this chapter).

At the very least, you can take it to the bank to earn a little interest instead of leaving it in cash. If you saw $10 laying on the ground, would you pick it up? Probably. Why not keep your $1,000 in the bank where it might earn that $10 or more for you? Doing otherwise is like walking right past that ten-dollar bill.

Compound interest: 1% example

Interest rates fluctuate, but for our example let's assume you can get 1% at the bank with virtually no risk of losing your money. Here's the math behind figuring out what you would make on 1%:

> *1% is the same as 0.01*
>
> *$1,000 Invested x0.01 Interest = $10 Earned*
>
> *End of Year 1 Balance = $1,000 + $10 = $1,010*

A shortcut to get to the final balance is to add 1 to the interest number, as shown below:

> *$1,000 x 1.01 = $1,010*

Now let's assume you can get 1% a year for 10 years—nice round numbers. Keep in mind, you will also earn interest on your interest. Your second year, you aren't multiplying your interest rate by $1,000. You are multiplying by $1,010.

	Ending Balance
Year 2 = $1,010.00x 1.01	$1,020.10
Year 3 = $1,020.10 x 1.01	$1,030.30

Year 4 = $1,030.30 x 1.01 $1,040.60

Year 5 = $1,040.60 x 1.01 $1,051.01

Year 6 = $1,051.01 x 1.01 $1,061.52

Year 7 = $1,061.52 x 1.01 $1,072.14

Year 8 = $1,072.13 x 1.01 $1,082.86

Year 9 = $1,082.85 x 1.01 $1,093.69

Year 10 = $1,093.68 x 1.01 $1,104.62

Yr	Begin	Interest	Ending Balance
1	$1,000	$10.00	$1,010.00
2	$1,010	$10.10	$1,020.10
3	$1,020	$10.20	$1,030.30
4	$1,030	$10.30	$1,040.60
5	$1,041	$10.41	$1,051.01
6	$1,051	$10.51	$1,061.52
7	$1,062	$10.62	$1,072.14
8	$1,072	$10.72	$1,082.86
9	$1,083	$10.83	$1,093.69
10	$1,094	$10.94	$1,104.62

After 10 years, your balance is $1,104.62. You've earned $104.62 more than if you'd left it in the piggy bank. Would you leave $104.62 on the sidewalk if you saw it?

Compound interest: 2% example

Now, 10 years is a long time to wait for 100 bucks. I get it and I agree. There were days, and there may be days again, when you could earn more than 1% at the bank.

You can do other things to earn more on your money. If you don't mind giving up daily access to the money, you can buy a CD—a "certificate of deposit."

Nerd Word Alert

Certificate of Deposit: A cash investment offering a slightly higher rate than savings accounts, but requiring you to keep it in the account for a specified length of time.

Basically, it says you won't touch the money for a little while, and in exchange, the bank will pay you a little more interest. Generally, if you need to break your pledge, you have to give up your interest or pay a fee.

Let's assume for our example a 1-year CD pays 2%. Assume you can keep renewing that CD at 2% each year for 10 years. Let's see what that does to the numbers.

Yr	Begin	Interest	Ending Balance
1	$1,000	$20.00	$1,020.00
2	$1,020	$20.40	$1,040.40
3	$1,040	$20.81	$1,061.21
4	$1,061	$21.22	$1,082.43
5	$1,082	$21.65	$1,104.08
6	$1,104	$22.08	$1,126.16
7	$1,126	$22.52	$1,148.69
8	$1,149	$22.97	$1,171.66
9	$1,172	$23.43	$1,195.09
10	$1,195	$23.90	$1,218.99

At the end of 10 years, you have $1,218.99. You've earned $218.99 more than sticking it in the piggy bank. That's better than a stick in the eye, right? I think it's worth it.

Compound interest: 3% example

Just for fun let's start playing with the rates. Let's assume you can buy a

10-year CD that pays 3%.

Yr	Begin	Interest	Ending Balance
1	$1,000	$30.00	$1,030.00
2	$1,030	$30.90	$1,060.90
3	$1,061	$31.83	$1,092.73
4	$1,093	$32.78	$1,125.51
5	$1,126	$33.77	$1,159.27
6	$1,159	$34.78	$1,194.05
7	$1,194	$35.82	$1,229.87
8	$1,230	$36.90	$1,266.77
9	$1,267	$38.00	$1,304.77
10	$1,305	$39.14	$1,343.92

OK, now you're making a little money. Your $1,000 grew to $1,343.92. That's $343.92 in profit after 10 years.

Compound interest: 4% example for 15 years

Let's assume you are super patient and can wait even longer for your money. You can let it cook for 15 years and are able to earn 4%.

Yr	Begin	Interest	Ending Balance
1	$1,000	$40.00	$1,040.00
2	$1,040	$41.60	$1,081.60
3	$1,082	$43.26	$1,124.86
4	$1,125	$44.99	$1,169.86
5	$1,170	$46.79	$1,216.65
6	$1,217	$48.67	$1,265.32
7	$1,265	$50.61	$1,315.93
8	$1,316	$52.64	$1,368.57

9	$1,369	$54.74	$1,423.31
10	$1,423	$56.93	$1,480.24
11	$1,480	$59.21	$1,539.45
12	$1,539	$61.58	$1,601.03
13	$1,601	$64.04	$1,665.07
14	$1,665	$66.60	$1,731.68
15	$1,732	$69.27	$1,800.94

At 4%, for 15 years, your $1,000 grew to $1,800.94. You made $800.94 just by being smart with your money.

Fifteen years is a long time to wait for $800 bucks, especially when you're a kid. But there are things you can do to try to earn even more than 4% on your money—like buy stocks!

Fit people smiling

Before we move on, I need to make a disclaimer.

When you go to the gym, you see pictures on the wall of fit people smiling. They look beautiful and happy. We don't see pictures of people hunched over, red-faced and out of gas right after a grueling workout. We don't see them massaging out sore muscles. We see them happy and beautiful and smiling.

These next few sections on investment returns are just like pictures of fit people smiling. They don't tell you how hard it was to get that way. They show a smooth return which NEVER HAPPENS in stock investing. You can certainly earn the returns expressed by investing in stocks, but not in a straight line. These examples are simply to help you understand the power behind compound interest.

As I taught my kids, I did the same as I am here. I showed them positive returns to help illustrate the power of compound interest. While I didn't focus on negative returns and losses here, I will cover more in future chapters, since investing in stocks means losing money at some point in the process. That's where the psychology comes in. For now...the numbers.

From interest to dividends

You've seen examples from 1-4%. Let's crank things up a little. Let's see if you can earn 5% on your money.

I'll cover much more about stocks in the rest of the book, so if you don't understand everything, don't worry. Just focus on the numbers.

Stocks represent businesses, and owning stocks means owning a portion of that business. Many stocks pay a portion of the business's profits to the owners in cold hard cash known as a dividend. Some stocks pay a dividend rate of 5% or more per year—stocks like AT&T. The stock price will fluctuate, but the dividends don't fluctuate all that much.

Nerd Word Alerts

Dividend: A portion of profits paid in cash to shareholders. (More on dividends in Chapter 10.)

Bulls and Bears: If you think a stock will go up in price, you are a "Bull" or "Bullish." If you think a stock will go down in price, you are a "Bear" or "Bearish."

Every time you pay your cell phone bill, you help pay that 5% dividend to AT&T shareholders. Now we could debate the bulls and bears of AT&T's stock price, but I'm confident that over 10 to 15 years, you'll make your 5% dividend and maybe a little more or less on the stock.

Let's run the numbers like before, only use 5% for 15 years.

Yr	Begin	Dividend	Ending Balance
1	$1,000	$50.00	$1,050.00
2	$1,050	$52.50	$1,102.50
3	$1,103	$55.13	$1,157.63
4	$1,158	$57.88	$1,215.51
5	$1,216	$60.78	$1,276.28
6	$1,276	$63.81	$1,340.10
7	$1,340	$67.00	$1,407.10
8	$1,407	$70.36	$1,477.46

9	$1,477	$73.87	$1,551.33
10	$1,551	$77.57	$1,628.89
11	$1,629	$81.44	$1,710.34
12	$1,710	$85.52	$1,795.86
13	$1,796	$89.79	$1,885.65
14	$1,886	$94.28	$1,979.93
15	$1,980	$99.00	$2,078.93

After 15 years at 5%, your $1,000 has grown to $2078.93. You have made $1,078.93 in profit from dividends alone.

There you go kids! If you recall, we started this chapter by saying "I'm going to show you how to turn that $1,000 into $2,000 or more by the time you graduate college in 10 to 15 years." You've done it! If you want to do it faster, you need to earn a higher rate of return.

I encourage you to let the kids plug their own numbers into the spreadsheet and see the return for 10%. See what 15% or 20% pays. Those may not be returns you can realistically expect to earn year in and year out, but there will be years when stock investors earn high returns.

More importantly, your kids may eventually be approached about getting a credit card with high interest rates. You will want them to know how those numbers work *against* you too. Or as Einstein also said:

> "Compound interest is the eighth wonder of the world. He who understands it, earns it...he who doesn't...pays it."

Show them how you build the spreadsheet and encourage them to learn how to use Excel. Even if you've never used a spreadsheet before, it takes only a few simple commands that you can find in the Appendix to model quite a bit of math. You don't need to be good at math and you don't need to be good at computers. Once you learn a few simple tricks, you'll amaze yourself, and you'll amaze your kids with the power of compound interest.

Let's go back to our discussion with the kids. You've just shown them how to double their money in 15 years. Let's show them one more example.

Compound interest: 10% example for 15 years

Let's imagine you are really good investors, and you earn 10% for 15 years. (You would need to be really good, but stranger things have happened.)

Let's look at 10% for this example.

Yr	Begin	Interest	Ending Balance
1	$1,000	$100.00	$1,100.00
2	$1,100	$110.00	$1,210.00
3	$1,210	$121.00	$1,331.00
4	$1,331	$133.10	$1,464.10
5	$1,464	$146.41	$1,610.51
6	$1,611	$161.05	$1,771.56
7	$1,772	$177.16	$1,948.72
8	$1,949	$194.87	$2,143.59
9	$2,144	$214.36	$2,357.95
10	$2,358	$235.79	$2,593.74
11	$2,594	$259.37	$2,853.12
12	$2,853	$285.31	$3,138.43
13	$3,138	$313.84	$3,452.27
14	$3,452	$345.23	$3,797.50
15	$3,797	$379.75	$4,177.25

Your $1,000 turned into almost $2,600 after 10 years and almost $4,200 after 15 years. That is more than quadrupling your money in 15 years.

I'll admit 10% is too much to expect, but it can and does happen. I recommend most people run their financial plans to expect a 6-7% return from their stock investments. I also recommend that they accept that in any given year, a diversified stock portfolio may go down 50% in a year and individual stocks may go down more (or even to zero). That is the risk inherent in investing in stocks.

It is your behavior that determines whether you realize those losses or ride them out. Behavior during downturns in the market is the number one reason you will succeed or fail as an investor in the stock market.

I thought it would be difficult to teach kids to behave properly in market downturns, but I am happy to say my kids surprised me. They responded quite well to seeing their account values drop. I'll share more as we go, but as long as you hold stocks of good businesses for the long-term, you can ride out the bad years and earn a higher return.

Compound interest with annual additions

You have now seen what you can do with your $1,000 in a range of returns. Let's think about what you've done and what the future holds. You've managed to save and earn $1,000 over the last few years, but that's just your initial goal and you aren't done earning and saving.

Let's play with the numbers so you can see more evidence for Einstein's quote about compound interest being so powerful. We'll also add a little to our Excel skills.

Assume you're able to save an additional $100 a year. That's not unreasonable, and we can play with that number the way we played with interest rates. I'm running it at 5% because I think you can understand by now why you might as well stick it in AT&T for that dividend.

Yr	Begin	Interest	Additions	Ending Balance
1	$1,000	$50.00	$100.00	$1,150.00
2	$1,150	$57.50	$100.00	$1,307.50
3	$1,308	$65.38	$100.00	$1,472.88
4	$1,473	$73.64	$100.00	$1,646.52
5	$1,647	$82.33	$100.00	$1,828.84
6	$1,829	$91.44	$100.00	$2,020.29
7	$2,020	$101.01	$100.00	$2,221.30
8	$2,221	$111.07	$100.00	$2,432.37

9	$2,432	$121.62	$100.00	$2,653.98
10	$2,654	$132.70	$100.00	$2,886.68
11	$2,887	$144.33	$100.00	$3,131.02
12	$3,131	$156.55	$100.00	$3,387.57
13	$3,388	$169.38	$100.00	$3,656.95
14	$3,657	$182.85	$100.00	$3,939.79
15	$3,940	$196.99	$100.00	$4,236.78

In 10 years, earning only 5% and saving $100 a year, you have turned your $1,000 + $1,000 in additions ($2,000) into $2,886.68. That's $886.68 in profit. Would you leave $886.68 on the ground?

In 15 years, earning only 5% and saving $100 a year, $1,000 + $1,500 in additions ($2,500) your money turns into $4236.78. That's $1,736.78 in profit. I'm quite certain I'd pick up $1,736.78. But then again, I like money.

I have found with both kids and grown-ups, it helps to take things in small doses. $100 a year sounds like a ton of money to a kid. In reality, it equates to $8.33 a month or $1.92 a week. If I'm paying the child an allowance, these are numbers that are not out of reach.

Similarly, for adults, the thought of investing $5,000 in an IRA or Roth IRA might seem daunting. If you break it down, it is $416.66 per month or $96.15 per week.

I encourage all grown-ups to run the numbers on what $5,000 a year can do at various rates of return.

I also encourage you to see what that $5 a day Starbucks habit can do if you run the numbers on it as an investment: $5 a day is $1,825 per year.

One last example with annual additions

Let's run one more example, showing you saving $3 a week ($156 per year). I think we can do better than AT&T, so let's see what the numbers look like earning 7% interest.

Yr	Begin	Interest	Additions	Ending Balance
1	$1,000	$70.00	$156.00	$1,226.00
2	$1,226	$85.82	$156.00	$1,467.82
3	$1,468	$102.75	$156.00	$1,726.57
4	$1,727	$120.86	$156.00	$2,003.43
5	$2,003	$140.24	$156.00	$2,299.67
6	$2,300	$160.98	$156.00	$2,616.64
7	$2,617	$183.17	$156.00	$2,955.81
8	$2,956	$206.91	$156.00	$3,318.72
9	$3,319	$232.31	$156.00	$3,707.03
10	$3,707	$259.49	$156.00	$4,122.52
11	$4,123	$288.58	$156.00	$4,567.09
12	$4,567	$319.70	$156.00	$5,042.79
13	$5,043	$353.00	$156.00	$5,551.79
14	$5,552	$388.62	$156.00	$6,096.41
15	$6,096	$426.75	$156.00	$6,679.16

After 15 years, you would have invested $3,340.00 and earned $3,339.16 in profit. That's almost a perfect double!

If you're still a little fuzzy on all of this, don't fret. We haven't yet come to the chapters on investing in cash, bonds, and of course stocks. I just want you to see the power behind compound interest early in the book, to help you understand its power to earn you money. Stay with me and it will all become clearer as we build in each chapter.

The Rule of 72

Compound interest cannot be covered without explaining one of the coolest mysteries of compound interest: "The Rule of 72."

This rule is a way to estimate the number of years it would take to double one's money at a given rate of return.

Let's put the rule into action. How long will it take to double your money at a 7% interest rate?

> *72 ÷ 7 = 10.2 years*
>
> *(Calculated precisely, it takes 10.3 years for money to double at 7%.)*

How about 5%?

> *72 ÷ 5 = 14.4 years*
>
> *(Calculated precisely, it takes 14.2 years for money to double at 5%.)*
>
> *Pretty cool right?*

The Rule of 72 is a rough estimate rather than a specific calculation. It's a fast and easy way to get "good enough" numbers when you're evaluating investments. It's less accurate outside the 6-10% interest rate range.

To make specific calculations, use a financial calculator or spreadsheet such as Excel.

Inflation

For the purpose of our discussion, inflation is the idea that prices generally go up over time. Most of what we consume sees price inflation: food, communications, housing, education, and entertainment, as well as energy for heating, cooling, and transportation. There are more academic ways to define inflation, but this description is good enough for our discussions.

I recently talked to my dad on his 66th birthday. His insurance agent sent him a birthday card that showed him how much things cost in 1952, his birth year. A gallon of gas was 20 cents. The average home sold for $16,000.

Cost of Living in 1952	
New Home	$9,075
Average Income	$3,850 year
New Car	$1,754
Average Rent	$80 month
Movie Ticket	$0.70
Gasoline	$0.20 gallon
U.S. Postage	$0.03 ounce

Food	
Sugar	$0.09 pound
Milk	$0.97 gallon
Ground Coffee	$0.74 pound
Eggs	$0.25 dozen
Ground Beef	$0.53 pound
Fresh Bread	$0.16 loaf

His dad (my grandpa) owned a gas station in the small rural Kansas town where he grew up. My dad remembers price wars when he was young when a gallon of gas dropped to $0.10 a gallon.

Remember my story about one of my first purchases with my own money being a candy bar that cost $0.30 in 1983. I watched that turn into $0.40, then $0.50. Today that bar will cost you 75 cents to $1.00.

My first concert was Aerosmith in 1989. I paid $20 for the ticket. That same level of show would cost $100 today. Interestingly, the T-shirt I bought at the show cost $30 (a ridiculous amount at the time). Today, that same shirt cost about...$30. Wait...*what*? Why is that?

Not everything we purchase sees price inflation; "Deflation" is the opposite of inflation.

Compared to today's price to see Aerosmith, the price of the T-shirt didn't increase much for many reasons, but I'm happy to speculate a little bit as to why. For one, Aerosmith the band is "made in America" and can't just be reproduced anywhere, while the T-shirt is likely made in another country with a much lower cost of labor. Over time, products that can be created anywhere tend to have less price inflation. You can produce T-shirts anywhere you can put a factory and find low-wage labor.

But there's only one Aerosmith, and the cost to see them has price inflation.

Technology is another thing that generally sees price deflation over time.

Sony introduced the first videocassette recorder (VCR) in 1975, at a list price of $1,400. By the time I was a kid in 1984, the price was cut by nearly two-thirds, to about $500.[1] The Motorola DynaTAC, the first cell phone on the market, was priced at $3,995 in 1983 and could only make phone calls. Not one game on it. Now we pay hundreds of dollars for that little computer in our pocket called a smartphone.

This is an over-simplification of inflation, but I do it to illustrate a point. As you think about investing and buying stocks, you should think about the price of things. You'll want to know a little about the prices of what a company is selling. Will they be able to keep that price level or will shifts in demand force them to change? What about the prices a company must pay to purchase the materials to create its product? There may be price fluctuations to consider from that angle as well.

With our music example, there have been a lot of moving parts in the music business since my first concert 30 years ago. The internet, and eventually smartphones, transformed how artists make money, and whether they could make money at all. People switched from buying albums to individual songs. As CD album sales faded, you saw live music become a larger portion of income for artists.

Side note: Begin to think about the businesses involved in these changes and think about them as if you owned them. From the artists to the record companies to the record stores—to the technology companies that disrupted them—there are business stories to be told.

Looking at the Radio Shack ad above, think about the technology stories it tells. Or maybe a business story comes to mind. You don't see many Radio Shack stores these days, do you?

Since the price of most things we spend generally rises over time, $1 today buys more than it will years from now. If we take our savings and just put it in a safe, it won't be worth as much in the future. It might buy you a whole candy bar today, but only half a candy bar in 24 years. We need to invest our money because who wants only half a candy bar?

Note

1) "Innovations Spur Boom in VCR Sales," The New York Times, Nov. 12, 1984

7 | The Most Important Rule in Investing

If I were to ask a room full of financial advisors what the most important rule in investing is, I would probably get two answers right away: "Buy low and sell high" and "Diversification" (aka, don't keep all your eggs in one basket).

Those rules are important, but not the most important rules in investing.

Buy low, sell high is just too generic to be useful. If we knew it was high or low, don't you think we would do just that? Diversification is certainly important, but it doesn't quite get to the point I want to drive home.

I don't really want to say that everyone is wrong and that I'm right...but maybe I will anyway. Most experienced financial planners agree with me once they hear the rule. In my experience, if this rule isn't followed, none of those other rules even matter.

OK, so enough already. The rule please:

Don't Invest in Long-Term Investments for Short-Term Goals

Put another way: Have a proper *time-horizon* and *goal* in mind for every investment. And if you don't have an emergency cash reserve, that's your first goal.

Nerd Word Alert

Time Horizon: The length of time until you are expecting to need the money you are investing.

It is imperative to match the type of investment you are choosing with your goal and the time horizon of when you will need to access your money.

Stocks are always long-term investments. They need a minimum time horizon of five years, but longer is better. Cash and bonds can be structured as long or short-term investments.

If you'll need the money soon or right away, don't buy long-term investments.

The first questions any good financial planner will ask you before investing your money should be, "What is the goal or plan for this money? When do you need to access it again? Is there a reason you might need to access the money before that time?"

A good financial planner is always playing "what if" with your life. They think about "what if this happens?" or "what if this goes wrong?" What would you do?

If the answer to "what would you do" is beg, borrow or steal, it means your first financial goal should be a cash reserve. You have little business investing towards long-term goals if you haven't addressed your short-term needs. The foundation of a financial plan is adequate reserves. I'm not saying you shouldn't begin to invest at all unless you have *fully* funded your reserves, but you certainly need to address savings on some level before thinking about long-term investments and goals.

If you haven't set aside enough cash for when the inevitable things go wrong in life, it can make you a bad investor out of no fault of your own, and here's why: If you haven't addressed your short-term needs and goals adequately, you may find you have to sell your stocks or bonds at a bad time to address an emergency situation.

Life is going to throw you not just curveballs, but expensive curveballs. You can't deal with them and keep your long-term investments in place through sell-offs and bear markets if you aren't prepared for the curve.

If we are a bad transmission or broken water heater away from having to sell our stock and bond portfolio, then we probably don't have enough reserves. We are in danger of having to sell our stock when *life* wants us to instead of when *we* want to.

If I know that my investment is long-term and there is very little chance of needing to access the money, it keeps me in the proper frame of mind to be successful as an investor. It keeps my expectations grounded. We will talk extensively about expectations and trying to stay grounded when we discuss "Stock Picking" in Chapters 11-15.

You will inevitably have periods of time when the market—or a stock—is going the wrong way. If you follow the rule of long-term investments for long-term goals, it may keep you from selling low. You're more likely to stay the course and ride out the down times if you are reminding yourself, "I don't need this money for 10 years."

8 | Intro to Investing: Money Trees

Think of each of your investments as money trees, each with its own purpose. Some trees you plant to produce fruit. Some trees you plant to provide shade or shelter. Investments are the same way; they are each different and serve different purposes.

When it comes to saving money at the kid level, you have three basic tree types or "asset classes" to choose from: cash, bonds, and stocks.

This is really important: *Cash is cash. Bonds are loans. Stocks are ownership.*

> ### Nerd Word Alerts
>
> **Asset**: Something of value that can be sold.
>
> **Asset Class**: A group of assets with similar characteristics.
>
> **Cash**: An investment that you can get to relatively quickly with almost no risk of loss.
>
> **Bond**: A type of loan to an entity that can be bought or sold by investors.
>
> **Stock**: Shares of ownership in a company that can be bought or sold by investors.
>
> **Real Estate**: Land and buildings.

For the majority of grown-ups, their choices for investments aren't too much different. They may add a fourth asset class with real estate, but even that is far from the majority.

You can own real estate as your primary residence (in which case I would more accurately call it an expense, but that discussion is beyond this book) or you can own rental property (which I would agree to call an investment).

If you're dealing with a sufficient amount of money, a case can be made for teaching kids to buy real estate, but that is not a topic for this book. (And my kids couldn't pull that kind of allowance.)

Going back to our tree analogy, cash and bonds are your fruit and nut producing trees. They produce my favorite types of fruits and nuts— MONEY! They produce money in the form of cash income paid to the owner. Later on, if you need your money, you can sell your tree for cash.

Stocks are your big beautiful shade trees and big beautiful forests. You can plant one small tree and watch it grow bigger and bigger. One tree can lead to many, which leads to a whole forest of trees.

Risk and Reward

Low risk, low reward: High risk, high "potential" reward. That's how money works.

With our three asset classes, you can make and lose the most in stocks, the least in cash, and bonds are in the middle.

Bonds represent loans to an entity; stocks represent ownership in an entity.

With a loan, the most you can ever make is getting paid back on the loan plus the interest you charge. When you own, your fortunes follow the fortunes of the business—both good and bad. If the company does well, the owners share in the profits. If the company does poorly, the owners get paid last. Note that corporate bondholders have priority over stockholders in the event of a "bankruptcy."

> ### Nerd Word Alert
>
> **Bankruptcy**: A federal court procedure that helps businesses settle debts and repay creditors, protecting them from creditors through the process. Bankruptcies can have either reorganization or liquidation as the objective.

If a company goes out of business and they sell all the assets of the business in a liquidation, the remaining cash (if there is any) after paying employees, vendors, etc., goes to the bondholders before the stockholders. In a typical liquidation, bondholders usually get only pennies on the dollar while stockholders won't get any residual value.

Sometimes a company will file bankruptcy and then reemerge as a new entity. General Motors (GM) is one recent example of a well-known company declaring bankruptcy, then returning to have a decent business.

GM declared Chapter 11 bankruptcy in June 2009, then emerged on July 2009 as a new company, which was majority owned by the U.S. Treasury through an elaborate bailout plan. The company may have emerged, and is on solid footing today, but the investors in GM bonds before the bankruptcy lost the majority of their investments and the stockholders took a total loss.

Truth be told, my kids don't know what a bond is. We skipped straight to stocks once they saved their cash cushions. They have plenty of time before they'll need their money, and they want to make the highest return we can, so they bought stocks.

As you will discover in the next few pages, cash and bonds are quite boring, even though they are quite necessary. I'll try to keep it interesting.

Cash is cash

Paper bills and coins are certainly cash, but *not* the best way to "store" your extra cash. Theft, fire, loss, accessibility—there are plenty of reasons not to keep too much cash sitting around the house. When I talk about cash, I'm referring to going to a bank or similar location and depositing your money.

Cash is the fruit tree with a money-back guarantee for life. It only gives you a small harvest of cash, but you can get your money back at any time for any reason.

Cash investments are almost always guaranteed by a government program such as the Federal Deposit Insurance Corporation (FDIC), up to a certain amount.

Cash should *always* be your first investment. My kids didn't start buying stocks until they had $500 saved in a savings account.

Stocks and bonds fluctuate in price, and cash does not. Cash is there to dip into, so you don't have to sell your stocks and bonds at a bad time (aka when they are down).

If you put $500 into a cash account at the bank, you'll have at least $500 when you go to get it. Now $500 might not buy as much stuff from one year to the next (as we saw in our inflation discussion), but you'll have your $500. The same cannot be said for stocks and bonds. Sometimes you have to ride out bad times in the stock and bond market.

Remember from Chapter 7: If you don't have good cash reserves, you set yourself up for failure as an investor.

There are different types of cash investments that provide a higher or lower rate of return based on how quickly you need access. More "liquid" investments will provide less return.

Nerd Word Alert

Liquidity: A measure of how quickly you can turn invested money into cash. The more "liquid" an investment, the more quickly it can be turned into cash without adverse consequences.

Savings and money market accounts are typically your first cash accounts and may offer a small interest rate. You can typically access your money immediately with an ATM or debit card.

Certificates of Deposit, or CDs, offer a slightly higher rate of return than savings and money market accounts. For your higher rate of return, you'll need to agree to leave the money invested for a certain length of time, usually from six months to several years. The longer you agree to not touch the money, the higher the interest rate the bank will pay. Should you need to access the money before the time is up, there may be a penalty, but more commonly you would forgo any interest earned.

Bonds are loans

Bonds are loans to whatever entity is issuing the bond. If a company (or government entity) for whatever reason doesn't want to borrow from a bank, they may choose to issue bonds to investors instead. If the U.S. government is issuing the bond and you purchase it, you're loaning your money to the government.

In return for the loan, the entity will agree to pay you interest as well as pay the loan back eventually. You also have the option to sell the bond or loan before the "term" is up to another investor if you want to.

In our tree analogy, bonds are fruit and nut trees that produce cash twice a year, then at the end of their life, they pay you back at whatever price they started their life. But in this case, if you want your money back before the end of their life, you have to find someone to buy the tree. There's no money-back guarantee.

Nerd Word Alerts

Par: Usually $1,000 per bond. The amount the bond issuer must pay back to a bond investor. "At par" means at $1,000.

Term: The amount of time until the bond or loan must be paid back. A 20-year term bond will be paid in 20 years.

Maturity: The date the company (or entity) is obligated to pay the $1,000 back to investors.

Coupon: The interest payment on a bond. The term originated when bonds were issued in paper form and you would tear off a "coupon" from the bond twice a year and trade it in for cash.

Bonds are typically issued in $1,000 increments, meaning each bond represents a $1,000 loan to the company. Bonds are issued with "maturities" from as short as 30 days to as long as 30 years, or even longer.

Bond issuers typically pay interest or "coupons" on bonds twice a year (semiannually). A 5% coupon bond would pay 5% of $1,000 in cash or $50. Broken into semiannual payments, that's $25 every six months

Types of bonds
Within the bond universe, we have various major types of bonds:

- U.S. Treasury Bonds: Issued by the U.S. government, these are considered the safest bonds in the world.
- Foreign Government Bonds: Issued by other countries to finance government operations.
- U.S. Municipal Bonds: Issued by city, state, and local governments. There are many varieties and nuances

in the "muni" world. Some are riskier than others, but many are very safe and may receive preferential tax treatment.

- U.S. Corporate Bonds: Issued by U.S.-based corporations. There are thousands of complexities and nuances. Stronger companies pay lower rates, weaker companies pay higher rates. Even within bonds from the same company you may see several bond types.

A typical bond issue example
A bond issue may look something like this:

- $1,000 bond issued at par
- 5% coupon ($25 twice a year)
- Maturity in 20 years

If you bought this bond when it was issued, you would have paid $1,000. The issuer would pay you $25 twice a year ($50 per year) for 20 years. After 20 years, you would get your $1,000 back.

What happens if you want your money back before 20 years? You have to sell it to someone else, and they may give you more or less than $1,000 for the bond. They may give you a "premium" or they may want a "discount" on it depending on how the risks have changed.

A bond priced below $1,000 (par) is trading at a discount. If it is trading for $900, it has a $100 discount.

A bond that is priced above $1,000 (par) is trading at a premium. If it is trading for $1,100, it has a $100 premium.

Why do the prices change? Expectations changed. We will discuss expectations extensively in future chapters. Changes in expectations cause changes in prices. That's the risk in investing your money instead of leaving it in cash.

With bonds, there are two primary expectations that drive the prices above or below $1,000. Expectations regarding getting paid back (credit), and expectations around what interest rates will look like in the future. I'll discuss both below.

When you buy your bond from the issuer that is called buying in the "primary market". When you sell it to another investor, that's called selling in the "secondary market." Neither are actual locations, just generic terms distinguishing who is selling the bonds.

Nerd Word Alerts

Premium: Bonds trading higher than their par value.

Discount: Bonds trading lower than their par value.

Credit Risk: The risk that you don't get paid back.

Interest Rate Risk: The risk that interest rate changes cause your investments to change in price.

Primary Market: Buying bonds or stocks directly from a company, government or issuing entity.

Secondary Market: Buying bonds or stocks from other investors after they've been issued by a company, government or entity. Most transactions for individual investors occur in the secondary market.

Credit risk is a nerdy way of saying "oops." Something went wrong somewhere along the way with the issuer since the time you bought the bond. New information has come to light. Perhaps whoever you loaned money to is potentially going to have a harder time paying you back than you originally thought. It might all turn out just fine and dandy, but it might not. If you are trying to sell your bond to someone, whoever is buying it today will want a discount.

In our tree analogy, maybe bad weather caused our tree to stop producing fruit, so we can't sell it for $1,000 anymore.

Credit risk can also work in your favor. If you bought a bond when things didn't look so hot for a company or entity, they probably had to pay you a higher interest rate to get the loan. Maybe it has a 7% coupon instead of 4% because things looked a little sketchy for the company. Or maybe the bond was already at a discount and you bought it in the secondary market.

In our tree analogy, maybe we got a good deal on a tree that everyone thought was going to die, but it regained health and produced fruit!

In either case, you can potentially earn a higher return by taking more risk. It's always "potentially" in investing. If it were a sure thing, it wouldn't be a risk, and you wouldn't get paid more for it. You know what a sure thing is called? It's called CASH.

Interest rate risk can be harder to understand. Let's use a savings account as an example.

Interest rates on savings accounts, CDs, mortgages, etc., change all the time as the economy changes and the business world turns. The reasons for these changes are too many to cover in this book, but know that interest rates move up and down just like the price of gas.

Let's use our bond example from above. We had a 5% bond for 20 years issued at $1,000 par. Assume the bond is being issued by a relatively large U.S. company on solid financial footing. There is little reason to believe the company won't pay back the bond, as they always have for decades.

Assume your local banks, on the same day this bond was issued, are offering a five-year CD for 2.5%. This means you would get 2.5% for the next 60 months on cash, or 5% on this bond. You buy the bond because you like money.

Now fast forward five years. For whatever reason, interest rates have moved, and now you can get a five-year CD at the bank for 5%. You still have 15 years left on this bond before you get your $1,000 back, but CD buyers can get the same rate guaranteed for five years.

You may find it hard to get your $1,000 for your bond if investors can buy a CD and get the same rate as your bond's coupon. That's interest rate risk. Fluctuations in interest rates can make your bonds more or less attractive to other buyers.

Keep in mind that even if the price of your bond drops due to risks, if you hold it to maturity, you'll get your $1,000 back (assuming no bankruptcy).

Current Yield

Most bonds are bought and sold in the "secondary market," therefore most bonds are not bought or sold at par. They almost always will have a premium or discount associated with them.

It can be difficult to know whether a 5% coupon bond is a good deal or not if you pay more or less than $1,000 for it. You will still get your $50 coupon each year, but no matter what you paid for the bond, you're only getting $1,000 back at maturity. The actual interest you earn on your investment will be lower or higher than the 5% coupon depending on if you buy the bond for more or less than $1,000 par.

If you pay $1,100 for the bond, you are taking a $100 loss at maturity. If you pay $900 for the bond, you're making a $100 gain on the bond at maturity.

To calculate the actual yield you'll earn on a bond that is not priced at par of $1,000, divide the coupon by the current price of the bond in the market. This is known as "current yield."

Nerd Word Alert

Current Yield: The annual yield earned on a bond at the current market price.

A bond with a 5% coupon ($50) trading in the secondary market at $1,100 has a current yield of:

$50 coupon ÷ $1,100 current market price = 0.0454
or 4.54%

The 4.54% figure is what you will actually earn annually on your money if you hold the bond to maturity. That is less than the 5% coupon.

Let's change the numbers and assume the same bond is trading at a discount. You're able to buy it at a discount of $900.

A bond with a 5% coupon ($50) trading in the secondary market at $900 has a current yield of:

$50 coupon ÷ $900 current price = 0.0556 or 5.56%

The 5.56% figure is what you will actually earn on your money each year if you hold the bond to maturity. That is more than the 5% coupon.

Pricing of bonds

All things being equal, longer maturity bonds will typically pay a higher interest rate than shorter maturities. This is similar to CDs where the longer the maturity, the higher the rate. This is logical. If I'm going to have to wait longer to get my money back, you'll have to pay me more in return.

Bonds issued by the U.S. government can be considered as safe as an insured CD in terms of getting par back at maturity, but you still have the risk that you may have to sell prior to maturity for more or less than you paid.

The more "credit-worthy" the bond issuer, the lower the coupon or interest rate they have to pay to issue bonds. The higher the risk that the issuer won't be able to pay back the bond, the higher the interest rate they'll have to pay.

This is logical and no different than individuals borrowing money from a bank. If you apply for a mortgage or car loan or credit card, would you expect your rate to be higher or lower if you have good or bad credit? The better your credit rating, the lower your interest rate. The same goes for bonds.

That does it for our fruit and nut producing trees known as cash and bonds. Finally, it's time to enter the wonderful world of ownership—the wonderful world of stocks!

9 | Basics of Stocks 101: The Lemonade Stand

In 1952, when a reporter for The American Weekly asked criminal Willie Sutton why he robbed banks, he said, "That's where the money is."

Why do we buy stocks? Because that's where the money is! We can earn a higher return on stocks than we can on cash or bonds. A higher return means more money. Who wants more money? I do! I do!

So, what is a stock anyway?

Very simply, stocks represent ownership in a company or business.

I know it may seem much more complicated than that, but the basics are no different than if you and a friend open a lemonade stand together and each invest $50. You are both 50 percent owners in that business the same way you share ownership in publicly-traded stocks.

A "share" of stock represents a unit of ownership in that company or business. It is simple to know, but easy to forget that stocks represent real people and real businesses trying to make it in the world.

Nerd Word Alerts

Share: A unit of ownership for a company. Think of your "share of the company."

IPO (Initial Public Offering): The process of becoming publicly traded.

If you own stock in a company, you are a fractional owner in that business. You are, in essence, a "silent partner."

When you own stock in public companies, it is most likely a very, very small portion of the ownership of that business, but nonetheless, it still represents a voting ownership in that company.

You will even be notified with a request to vote your percentage of ownership at the annual meeting or online. You have a small vote, but really no influence on how the company is run. That's why I say you're like a silent partner.

Technically, if you were to buy so much company stock (hundreds of millions or billions of dollars) you could have enough ownership to influence the operations of the company. (For now, we'll leave that for the next book, Teaching Kids Corporate Takeovers.)

Publicly traded

As discussed previously, not all companies are available for the general public to buy on public exchanges. The examples I've used so far have been companies that are publicly traded. This means that as long as the markets are open and you have a stock brokerage account, you can purchase shares of these companies.

There are many reasons why a company may or may not want to be publicly traded.

Publicly-traded companies are formed under different regulations and laws compared to private companies and have very different financial reporting requirements.

Not every company wants to go through that kind of short-term scrutiny for their long-term plans. The stock market can be quite unfriendly and even shortsighted when it doesn't like a company's results or plans. At the same time, being publicly traded exposes a company to a larger pool of potential investors than they might be able to find without "going public."

There are very large companies that are still privately owned. Examples you may know include Uber, Airbnb, and other famous names from Silicon Valley. Those companies are owned by their founders and other private investors who provided initial funding. Your kids most likely are fans of Lego building sets and movies. Lego is also privately held, including much of it by the original family founders. But Lego theme parks are owned by another company called Merlin Entertainments, which is public (symbol MIINF).

Most of the world's diamond production is privately owned, including the DeBeers Group of Companies. In the realm of politics, we've often heard of the Koch brothers. Most of the money contributed to the candidates they support comes from Koch Industries, a multinational conglomerate that is the second largest private company in the U.S. The largest private company is Minnesota-based Cargill with revenues of well over $100 billion, which is still 90-percent owned by descendants of founder William Cargill and his son-in-law.

It's usually quite an exciting day for a company when they hit the market with an IPO. Many times, you may see quite wild price swings as the private shareholders take advantage of being able to sell, and the public investors take advantage of their first chance to own the company.

Lemonade Inc.

Let's go back to that lemonade stand analogy from the beginning of the chapter. Assume you and your best friend decide to start a lemonade stand. She has $50 to contribute, and you have $50 you've saved up from an old childhood bet with your dad. You decide to call it Lemonade Inc. because it sounds fancy and official to put Inc. in the name of things.

We will use your company, Lemonade Inc., as an example as we compare it to another popular fruit company called Apple Inc. This comparison will help demystify many of the numbers, letters, lines, and nerd words associated with the stock market.

The quote

Let's begin by pulling up a quote for Apple stock.

Remember from Chapter 1 that every stock has a symbol to represent it on the market. For Apple, the symbol is AAPL. If you go to a website or app that delivers stock quotes, you will see a field where you can type the ticker symbol. Below is a quote for Apple from Yahoo Finance.

There's a lot of information here. Let's focus on one number for now:$157.85.That's the most recent price for one share of AAPL stock at the end 2018.

If it's Monday through Friday between 6:30 a.m. and 1:00 p.m. PT, that price will be constantly changing. You may be amazed to see how much a stock price fluctuates during market hours.

These day-to-day, minute-by-minute fluctuations in stock prices occur as buyers and sellers are connected in the marketplace at different prices.

Once again, let's go back to that $157.85 number. If that's what one share is worth, how much is the whole company worth? I'm glad you asked. The answer is hidden next to the nerd word "Market Cap": $749 billion. Market cap equals the share price multiplied by the total number of shares issued.

Nerd Word Alert

Market Capitalization (market cap): The total value of a company. Calculated by multiplying the total shares by the share price.
MC = (share price) x (total shares)

On this particular day, the total value of Apple Inc. added up to approximately $749 billion.

Here's how the math works (rounding the numbers above):

$749 billion market cap ÷ $158 per share = 4.74 billion shares

or

$158 per share x 4.74 billion shares = $749 billion market cap

Lemonade Inc. on the other hand has 2 shares of stock, each worth $50 per share, giving it a total market cap of $100. (Hey, it has to start somewhere.)

There you go. Now you know what market cap means. It's the same as saying "the total value of the company."

More quote screen info

For the curious, below is a brief description of other items you see on the quote screen:

- Open: The first price at the most recent open of trading.
- Close or Previous Close: The price at the most recent close of the market.
- Day's Range: The high and low price for the current or most recent business day.
- 52 Week Range: The high and low price for the last 52 weeks. Sometimes you will see them quoted as 52 Week High and 52 Week Low.
- Small Chart: Notice that you can adjust the time frame in the chart to show the last day (1D), 5D, one month (1M), 6M, year to-date (YTD), one year (1Y), 5Y, or full history of the stock (Max).

For now, just ignore anything on the quote that we haven't covered. By the end of the next chapter, most of these terms will be familiar.

10 | Basics of Stocks 201: Simplifying Key Concepts

This is a very important chapter. We cover quite a bit of ground. Once you get through it, you'll be ahead of most of the public when it comes to understanding stocks.

We are going to continue to use Lemonade Inc. to help you understand the numbers behind Apple Inc. We'll continue to refer to the Apple chart in Chapter 9.

Earnings aka Profits

When you hear "earnings" think "profits." When it comes to stocks, good profits usually mean a good stock price. "Stocks follow earnings" is something I was taught long ago. It refers to the fact that stock prices tend to follow the same path as company earnings over the long term. More on that in Chapter 12.

Public companies report financial results quarterly, including earnings. Results are made public and executives usually provide a conference call in which they report the results of the previous quarter and discuss the state of the current business.

Earnings = Sales - Expenses

The rules of accounting and taxation make the actual calculation much more complicated than this, but for our purposes, the simple formula will work just fine.

Let's use the previous example from Lemonade Inc. One summer day you and your partner sell $100 worth of lemonade.

That means you have sales or "revenue" of $100.

> ### Nerd Word Alert
>
> **Revenue**: Another word for sales.

If you had total expenses for lemons, sugar, and supplies of $40, then you have earnings of $60.

$100 revenue - $40 expenses = $60

Earnings per Share = Total earnings ÷ Total shares

It is much easier to analyze data on a "per share" basis, as every company has a different number of shareholders. It makes it easier to compare data across multiple companies if we use per share numbers, like earnings per share.

To calculate earnings per share, or EPS, simply take total earnings and divide by the number of shares.

For Lemonade Inc., based on your earnings of $60, your "earnings per share" would be $30.

$60 earnings ÷ 2 shares = $30 EPS

EPS is one of the numbers on the Apple chart in Chapter 9. Notice that AAPL earned $11.91 per share for the 12 months prior to this quote.

So how much did AAPL make in total? I'm glad you asked.

Total earnings for Apple are not on the quote screen, but we can back into the numbers. Remember we calculated total shares of 4.74 billion in Chapter 9.

4.74 billion shares x 11.91 EPS = $56.45 billion

That's $56.45 billion in *profit*. In *one year*! That's a lot of apples.

Dividends and Retained Earnings

When a company makes money, they have to decide, "Do we leave the money in the business or reward shareholders by paying them back?"

Investors like to be paid back. They also like to see the companies they invest in succeed and do well. They don't want the company to fail because they paid the shareholders back too much or too quickly. It is one of the critical decisions executive managers make in running the business.

Going back to the Lemonade Inc., let's assume you and your fellow shareholder decide you want to keep $40 of your profits in the business to pay for the next round of lemons, sugar, and supplies. You decide to take the other $20 in cash for your own personal use (just like a bond pays cash).

The $40 you kept in the business is known as the "retained earnings" for the business. The $20 cash payment is known as the "dividend" you received from your company.

Nerd Word Alerts

Dividend: Cash paid from a company to shareholders.

Dividend Yield: Dividend divided by share price. It represents the equivalent of interest on cash or coupon on a par bond.

Retained Earnings: The portion of earnings not paid out as dividends.

Here's how to calculate these three numbers:

Earnings = Retained Earnings + Dividend

Dividend = Earnings - Retained Earnings

Retained Earnings = Earnings - Dividend

For Lemonade Inc.: $60 earnings - $40 retained earnings = $20 dividend

Just as we did with earnings, let's divide our dividend by the number of shares to get "dividend per share."

$20 dividend ÷ 2 shares = $10 per share

That means each of us is taking $10 cash home to do with whatever we want. Think of it the same way you think about interest on cash investments or coupons on bonds. It's another money tree.

Dividend Yield = Dividend per share÷Share price

You may recall in Chapter 8 we calculated "current yield" for bonds by taking the coupon and dividing it by the "current price" for the bond. We do a similar calculation to get to "dividend yield" for a stock. Divide the dividend by the share price to get the yield for Lemonade Inc.

$10 div per share ÷ $50 share price = 0.2 = 20%

Calculating the yield gives us a helpful way to understand the portion of our investment that will produce cash or income. It helps us understand the portion of our stock investment that acts like a fruit or nut tree.

Apple Dividend and Yield

Apple pays a dividend, but not all companies do. In the U.S., companies that pay dividends usually pay them quarterly.

If you look at the quote for AAPL, you'll notice a section for "Forward Dividend & Yield" and the numbers $2.92 (1.87%). This means that AAPL is expected to pay $2.92 ($0.73 per quarter) per share over the next 12 months (forward means "next year"). That equates to a 1.87% yield, calculated the same way as for Lemonade Inc. (Don't worry about the rounding differences.)

$2.92 dividend ÷ $157.85 share price = 0.0185 = 1.85%

Dividend History

It's helpful to look at a company's dividend history. Yahoo Finance has an excellent tool for doing so with the "Historical Price" feature. Pull up a quote on Yahoo Finance, select "Historical Prices," then select "Dividends Only" for the time frame you want to research. You can see the payment history and note whether it's a consistent pattern and if it has increased or decreased over time.

The Yahoo Finance chart shows the Apple dividend history since 2015:

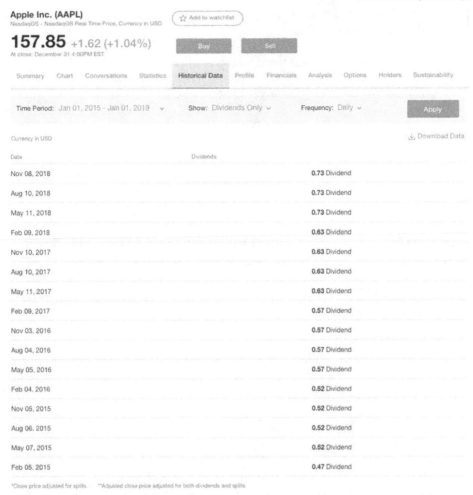

Notice how the dividend has increased since 2015. It started at $0.47 per share and has grown to $0.73 per share in a few years. That's a nice pay raise!

The Rosetta Stone of Financial Ratios

In a moment, I will share with you the "Rosetta Stone" of financial ratios. Perhaps that's a little strong, but it really does tell you a lot of information in a hurry. To keep you from flipping ahead, I'll let you know it is the Price/Earnings Ratio or the PE Ratio.

At this point, all the components of the ratio have been covered. Rather than work through an example, I'm going to explain why it matters before defining it for you.

Stay with me here—I've promised you the "Rosetta Stone" after all!

Let's go back to our example on dividend yield in the previous section.

Remember that to calculate the dividend yield, we need the current price per share. (dividend yield = dividend per share ÷ share price)

What's the share price of our Lemonade Inc? We have been using $50 per share because that's how much we each invested, and that is a reasonable number to use.

It is important to remember what we are *actually* calculating when we come up with a share price: the "value of the business."

Asking the question again: What is value of Lemonade Inc? Answer: "whatever someone will pay for it."

So, what might another investor pay? How do you value a business for sale or purchase? In reality, we're going to have a difficult time finding a buyer for our $100 annual revenue business, but what if we did? How might they value our business?

Remember, we talked about thinking about stocks as businesses. The same lessons apply from Lemonade Inc. to Apple Inc.

Typically, a buyer will offer "a multiple of annual profits." What's that mean? It means they will take annual profits and multiply it by a number and that will be the price they offer.

Nerd Word Alert

Multiple: The number of years of earnings (or sales or another metric) it requires to buy a business.

Another way to think of the multiple is: "How many years of earnings am I willing to pay up front."

Remember in Chapter 4 we discussed the show "Shark Tank"? You'll see this calculation in action if you watch it. It's one of the foundations of the offers as the Sharks negotiate with the business owners (and against each other) on the show.

What will that multiple number be? It depends on the business. The higher and more certain the growth prospects for the business, the higher the number. If the earnings stream is expected to stay flat or shrink, the number will be smaller. If many buyers are interested, the multiple will be higher. If hardly anyone is interested, the price will be lower. If the business is difficult to duplicate, the price will be higher. If the business is easy to duplicate, the price will be lower.

A prospective buyer will weigh all the positives and negatives of the business. They will likely compare other similar businesses that may have recently sold. At what multiple did that business sell and, based on similarities and differences, should this business be valued at a higher or lower multiple? That's what the buyer is trying to determine when making an offer.

Nerd Word Alert

Appraisal: The process for estimating how much an asset is worth in the market.

For those familiar with real estate, you may know the "appraisal" process. In this process, an appraiser will look at comparable properties and make adjustments based on those "comps." The same is true in business valuation; you compare similar businesses and make adjustments up or down based on the differences.

Assume one of the other neighbor kids, decides he wants to buy Lemonade Inc. from you and your best friend. He offers to pay you three times earnings or for three years of earnings up front. Earnings of $60 multiplied by three is $180 for the whole business, or $90 per share.

Another neighbor kid hears about the offer, she decides to out-bid him. She offers to pay four times earnings or for four years of earnings up front. Earnings of $60 multiplied by four is $240 for the whole business, or $120 per share.

Earnings x Multiple = Total Price (Market Cap)

or

Earnings per share x Multiple = Price per share

For Lemonade Inc.:

$60 in earnings x 3 (multiple) = $180 or $90 per share

$60 in earnings x 4 (multiple) = $240 or $120 per share

The formula we used in that calculation can be moved around thanks to the beauty of arithmetic.

Price = Earnings x Multiple

or

Multiple = Price ÷ Earnings

See what we have there? We have a Price ÷ Earnings ratio, a "PE Ratio." (We've covered some ground since starting this section on PE ratio, so this is a reminder.)

As you can see from this exercise, the PE ratio tells us how many years of earnings we are paying for up front for the business.

It tells us, if earnings stay the same, how many years before I'm paid back on my investment.

Nerd Word Alert

PE Ratio: Price per share÷ Earnings per share, aka the multiple. It is a ratio used to compare values of different companies compared to earnings.

Apple's PE ratio

For Apple, how many years of earnings do you need to pay up front? What's the multiple you would need to pay?

The answer is on the Apple chart in Chapter 9. The PE ratio is one of the numbers you'll see on most stock quotes. For Apple, the number is 13.25. That means the multiple is 13.25. You're paying for 13.25 years of earnings up front, given last year's earnings.

$157.85 Price ÷ 11.91 EPS = 13.25 years

It may have been a mystery number to you before. Or maybe you knew it was there, and that it meant price to earnings, but didn't realize it was The Rosetta Stone of Financial Ratios.

Wait a minute, I said that didn't I? I guess I need to explain why it is so important.

Applying the PE ratio

As you've seen, the PE ratio tells you how many years of earnings you need to pay up front for the stock today. That alone tells you a story about what the market thinks of that stock. If you know the market is willing to pay for 13.25 years of Apple earnings up front, it tells you something about stocks that trade at higher or lower PE ratios relative to Apple.

In one number, you find out what the market thinks of the growth prospects for the company, and you get a chance to decide if that makes sense or not. It provides a way to compare companies across market caps and industries in a uniform manner. More often, investors will compare the PE ratio of companies with similar businesses or to the average PE of a particular group of stocks.

Stock analysts will spend considerable time debating whether a stock is a "good value" or if the price is "justified." Typically, they are debating if the PE is too high or too low given the company's expected future earnings. In our examples, we used last year's earnings, but the market is trying to figure out what *future* earnings will look like.

For Apple, 13.25 might sound like a lot of years to pay for up front, but what if I told you Netflix has a PE of 101.5. That's right, over 100 years of earnings up front to buy Netflix. Obviously, investors expect earnings to grow to justify paying for 100 years of last year's earnings.

Comparing PE ratios

Let's dig a little deeper into the concept. Here's a hypothetical example of comparing two stocks.

Company A:

- Earnings last five years of $10 per share each year
- Projected earnings next five years are $10 per share each year
- Dividend is $1 per year

Company B:

- Earnings last five years of $0 per share each year
- Projected earnings next five years are $1, $5, $10, $20, $30
- Dividend – none

Which stock would you expect to have a higher PE ratio or multiple?

That all depends on how likely Company B is to achieve its earnings projections. The more the market believes those growth projections, the more likely the stock would have a pretty high PE ratio. If the market doesn't believe those numbers can be achieved, it may not pay much for the stock since the company hasn't shown any earnings yet.

What's the right price?

That's what the market tries to figure out every day, based on the information available.

Chapter 10 review

Chapter 10 covered a lot of ground. We started with a quote screen and by the end we were discussing the merits of company PE ratios!

If you were able to understand the examples relating to Lemonade Inc. and how they relate to Apple Inc., then you understand the concepts. Pat yourself on the back.

If you are still fuzzy, that's OK. Reread this chapter and Chapter 9, concentrating on the examples relating to Lemonade Inc. It may help your understanding to write down the number and math examples as you read.

We started by focusing on the stock price and understanding that it represents one share of an actual company. We discussed how earnings is another way of saying profits. The share of the profits paid out in cash is a dividend and the rest is retained earnings to run the business. We calculated dividends as a yield to help compare to other asset classes. To wrap it all up, we dove deep into the multiple and PE ratio and had a crash course on business valuation.

As you begin to think about stocks in the real world, start to pull up quotes on Yahoo Finance or another site. Look at the PE ratio on each one to begin to get a feel for how different stocks price. It will help you develop a sense of when things might be a good deal or not.

11 | Intro to Stock Picking 301: Story, Numbers, Expectations

Depending on the age of your kids, you may not be able to go through all the steps of the research process. I included enough depth in the book to help you teach yourself and your kids as much or as little as you need.

Feel free to keep it as simple or complex as you like.

Depending on the age of your children, it may just be a conversation that "Hey, this is the company that makes Frozen" and they say, "Yaaaaay Frozen." The process can start that simply.

As you walk through life, do what my kids and I did. We talked about good businesses we saw; we looked for a good *story*. We Googled whether they were publicly traded or not. We got into the numbers a little to see if they were profitable and to set our expectations correctly, then we pulled the trigger and bought. Then we didn't freak out. We didn't freak out because we set our expectations correctly. That's the process. Lather, rinse, repeat.

I'll dig deeper into each of these as we progress, but these three words summarize the stock picking process: Story, Numbers, Expectations.

- What's the story? What makes you want to own this business?
- What are the numbers? How much money are they making?
- What should our expectations be for the company and stock?

It is also a good time to point out, these aren't three individual steps we move through like we're following Lego instructions. Stock picking is not a simple math equation. These three steps represent themes that are woven together to help answer the first question: What's the story?

12 | Intro to Stock Picking 335: What's the Story?

Stocks are businesses

It can be overwhelming to think about narrowing the universe of stocks from over 10,000 to one. Let's keep it really simple.

Start by doing nothing but watching.

> "You can observe a lot by just watching." –Yogi Berra

Watch for good business. Watch for a good story.

When the kids and I talk about what stocks they might buy, we talk about it in terms of "what company or businesses do you want to own?" When you break it down, that's what you are really deciding when you buy a stock: Do you want to be an owner in that business?

Many of the biggest mistakes I've made with investing—and that I've seen others make—had to do with times when I forgot I was buying businesses. Times when I got sucked into chasing a stock that had been hot even though I didn't know much about it.

> "It is simple to know, but easy to forget, that stocks represent real people and real businesses trying to make it in the world."–J.J. Wenrich

What makes a good business? Look for companies you think are probably making money—selling lots of whatever it is they provide. The more the better.

It should be simple. You don't have to know that XYZ Company just made a new organic, solar-powered, Bluetooth-enabled, titanium, artificial heart valve. You just need to notice what *you* know and you understand in your everyday life.

Consider these quotes from Warren Buffett, aka The Oracle of Omaha. Buffett is one of the most successful investors in history and has repeatedly tried to tell the world that investing is much simpler than we make it:

> "If you have to go through too much investigation, something is wrong."

> "You don't need to be a rocket scientist to be a shrewd and successful investor."

> "There seems to be some perverse human characteristic that likes to make easy things difficult."

> "You should invest in a business that even a fool can run, because someday a fool will."

We should also buy what we understand, no matter what level of investor we are. "Buy what you know" is what I tell people.

Once you understand a business and how it makes money, it helps you develop a comfort level when the market moves against you. It will help prevent you from making a mistake with your money (which is a nice way of saying losing your money).

Buffett is known for owning quality companies for decades at a time:

> "Only buy something that you'd be perfectly happy to hold if the market shut down for ten years."

> "If you aren't willing to own a stock for ten years, don't even think about owning it for ten minutes."

What businesses do you see? What new trends have you noticed? Is there a company associated with that trend? What do you see in your day-to-day life that makes you say, "I wish I owned *that* business!" Do a little research and you might find you're able to own part of it.

People don't give themselves enough credit for recognizing great businesses when they see them. Your experiences matter. Your intuition matters. You're probably smarter than you think, and you very well could be earlier in a successful story and closer to an investment idea than you realize.

Many of the best stocks of this generation have been hidden in plain sight. We've been customers of some of the best companies—Amazon, Google, Apple, Netflix—but how many of us owned the stocks?

People have a tendency to think they are too late, when they are probably right on time if they would just act on what they see.

Sometimes people act, but when the stock goes down, they panic and sell for a loss after just a few days, weeks, or months. Then they never try again because they decide they're bad at it. (I cover more on this topic in Chapter 15.)

In the long run, they were likely right to buy the company, they just needed to give the investment more time. You probably aren't going to be in early enough that you catch the entire run up, but that doesn't mean you can't catch the rest of it. Stocks of good companies can run higher for a long, long time—years and even decades for the best ones.

So, give yourself credit. Maybe sometimes you *will* be too late but keep at it and you'll make enough on your winners to more than offset any losers.

"Line out the door" factor

Here's what I have observed by watching: If I see a line out the door of a business, it is worth investigating.

Raise your hand if you like waiting in line. I didn't think so. But if business is so good that people are waiting in line, there's an above-average chance you have a good business on your hands.

Think about the businesses in your life where there's a line out the door. Do you think they are doing good or bad business? If you answered good, then you might have homework to do.

"Nobody goes there anymore. It's too crowded."
–Yogi Berra

I've found a line out the door of *happy paying* customers gives you an above average chance at making money on that company's stock. In Chapter 17, I'll share the real-life stories to back it up, including one story about *unhappy* paying customers that helped me know a stock to avoid.

Are your companies publicly traded?

Begin to form a "watch list" of companies to investigate.

Many times, you might see something that makes you investigate only to find it's not publicly traded. You don't necessarily want to eliminate those companies from your list. You never know when it may go public in the future.

It can be a little tricky to find out which companies are public, like when it's a small part of a larger company. The smaller and less mainstream the idea, the harder it may be to find too.

Start by going to old faithful—Google. Search "is XYZ company publicly traded?" and see what you find. It may take you straight to Google Finance and a stock chart. Or to a link that answers your question (make sure to check the date).

You can also go to the company website and look for "about us," "investor relations" or "contact us" links at the bottom of the home page or through the site search. An investor relations link will generally tell you if it's public or private and provide the ticker symbol. Public companies like the world to know and have a "full disclosure" obligation to make investor information easily available. If you're having a difficult time finding investor relations, there's a higher likelihood that the company is privately-held.

Always be looking around the corner

One of my key reminders to myself in investing is to *always be looking around the corner*. You want to ask yourself questions about the future prospects for the company, What do I think will happen next?

The point in asking these questions is to think about where you see this business in three, five, or ten years.

Questions to consider:

- What do you know about the company?
- How do they make their money? (Do they make money?)
- Will they be making more or less in a few years?
- Are they part of a new trend that will continue or a fad that will last only a few years?
- Will other companies try to copy them and if so, can your company withstand the competition?
- Will the story last long enough for you to be a long-term stock investor?
- What could go wrong or right?

Don't try to talk yourself in or out of the investment. Do your best to take an objective view. You may find the process reinforces your position that you are onto something with your idea.

You just want to keep in mind that history is littered with companies that go from boom to bust because markets change every day just as tastes change. You want to make sure you aren't buying a fad right at the height of its popularity.

Certain businesses are more susceptible than others to changes in taste. Fashion can be very difficult to forecast years ahead because consumer tastes change so quickly. Certain brands have more staying power than others, but even strong brands miss on taste trends every now and then. Restaurants can be difficult to forecast for the same reason.

We discussed the line-out-the-door factor earlier and how that can be a good indicator of a good business. If you see a line out the door, you also want to ask yourself, "What will the line look like in 12 months?"

Stocks follow earnings

An old boss of mine used to begin every market update with the same line, "Well...stocks follow earnings...I expect companies will report good (bad) earnings so I expect the market will be good (bad) as well."

Then he would dig into why he thought earnings would be good or bad and discuss other factors that might move stocks. But at the end he would remind us again that other stuff doesn't really matter "unless it matters to earnings, because stocks follow earnings."

Remember, earnings means profits. Companies with good profits make good stocks. Companies with growing profits make *great* stocks!

This is where story and numbers begin to cross over each other. You want to find the story that will drive great numbers for a long time.

13 | Stock Picking 355: Numbers

Numbers keep you grounded

You've started on your stock's story, now let's continue and dig into the numbers. Don't worry, there are only a few numbers to discuss, and you've already learned most of the definitions and equations you need to know in previous chapters.

It can be easy to get caught up in the hype associated with a company, and the hype associated with investing, in general. Just seeing or hearing the words "get rich quick" can make your heart beat a little faster, even if you know better than to believe it.

Buying stocks can drive an adrenaline rush akin to gambling, especially if you approach it the wrong way by focusing on the short-term results. That rush can be quite addictive. It can force people to take on way too much risk and become self-destructive as they chase short-term results.

Many companies are good at not only promoting their business, but also promoting their stock through carefully-worded press releases and buzz words.

All of these things can impact your decision-making and make you forget that you're buying a business that you need to understand on a basic level.

The *numbers* can keep you grounded and focused on the fundamentals of long-term, buy and hold investing.

Earnings

Earnings can be found on most financial websites once you pull up a company's quote and other information. Examples include Google Finance, Yahoo Finance, cnbc.com, and Nasdaq.com.

You'll see the earnings for previous years or quarters and also a tab for Financials or Earnings.

The formats change from time to time, but I like to see the earnings in a graph or table. CNBC has a particularly nice format, shown below for Apple Inc.

Apple Inc.

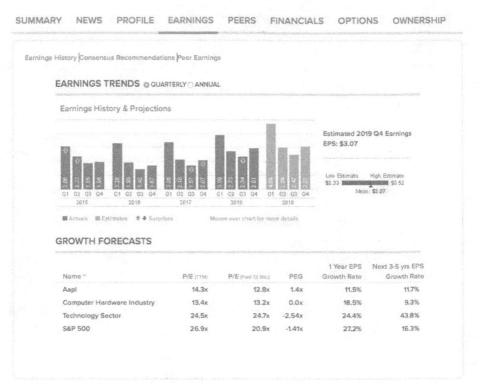

Again, stocks follow earnings over the long term. If the goal is to find stocks that go up, we probably want to see earnings that are going up. Makes sense, right?

Looking at earnings per share in table or graph form helps us understand: 1) What the earnings or losses have been, and 2) What the pace has been. Earnings over time tell a company's history.

AAPL has been able to grow their earnings per share from $9.22 in 2015 to $11.91 in 2018. In that same time (1/1/15 to 12/31/18), the stock price also went from $111.39 to $157.85 (including a little time above $230 in 2018).

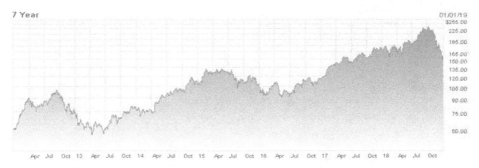

	High/Low Price	EPS
2012	100/57	6.31
2013	82/55	5.68
2014	119/70	6.45
2015	134/92	9.22
2016	118/89	8.31
2017	177/114	9.21
2018	233/146	11.91

You can also usually find earnings "projections" from the analysts who follow the company, as in the chart below from the Nasdaq site. Their "estimates for future earnings" help gauge whether the company is expected to grow and how quickly.

Nerd Word Alert

Earnings Projection: Estimates for future earnings per share from analysts that follow a company.

I recommend taking analyst projections with a grain of salt, as they are notoriously overly optimistic, but it will give you an idea of what the consensus expects.

87

Apple Inc. Earnings Forecast

$157.74 1.51 ↑ 0.97%

*Delayed - data as of Dec. 31, 2018   Find a broker to begin trading AAPL now

Exchange:NASDAQ
Industry: Technology
Community Rating: 🐦 Bullish

Yearly Earnings Forecasts

Fiscal Year End	Consensus EPS* Forecast	High EPS* Forecast	Low EPS* Forecast	Number of Estimates	Over the Last 4 Weeks Number of Revisions	
Sep 2019	13.18	13.86	11.11	13	1	4
Sep 2020	14.7	15.75	12.09	12	1	3
Sep 2021	16.11	18.07	13.13	4	0	0
Sep 2022	14.14	14.14	14.14	1	0	0

Quarterly Earnings Forecasts

Fiscal Quarter End	Consensus EPS* Forecast	High EPS* Forecast	Low EPS* Forecast	Number of Estimates	Over the Last 4 Weeks Number of Revisions	
Dec 2018	4.66	4.85	4.41	12	0	5
Mar 2019	2.96	3.19	2.34	11	1	4
Jun 2019	2.43	2.62	1.86	11	0	0
Sep 2019	3	3.28	2.46	11	1	0
Dec 2019	5.13	5.3	4.84	5	1	0

See also: AAPL Earnings Date

The *direction* of earnings

Given what you know about the story so far, what do you think the future path for earnings will look like? That's one of the most important questions in stock picking. We want to find companies that we feel can grow their earnings over time, as those are often the best investments over the long term.

Granted, a company may have to lose money at first, but that lasts only as long as you have money to stay in business. I'm also not saying you should never buy a company that has negative earnings (aka is losing money). Most companies start by losing money, and that's fine. We just need to understand that the risk of losses is higher when we buy companies that aren't making money yet.

Even some of the real-life stories I will share in Chapter 17 are stories of companies that were *losing* money not-so-very-long ago, but turned out to be fantastic investments over the long-term. I'll even eat a little humble pie and admit that I should have let Annabel buy a riskier stock than she did, as she would have made a *lot* more money by buying the company with less certain earnings.

Dividends

Dividends can be an important portion of your "total return" in a stock market investment.

Nerd Word Alerts

Total Return: The entire amount of money you make on an investment. For a stock, you earn cash dividends, as well as your capital appreciation or depreciation.

Capital Appreciation (Depreciation):The difference between what you paid for a stock and the unrealized or realized capital gain (loss).

Realized Capital Gain (Loss): The difference between the price you buy and sell. If you buy for $10 and sell for $15, you had a realized capital gain of $5.If you buy for $10 and sell for $8, you have a realized capital loss of $2.

Unrealized Capital Gain (Loss):For an asset you have *not* sold yet, the difference between the price you bought it for and the current market price. In other words, what your realized gain or loss would be if you sold it right now.

Total Yield: Your return as a percentage. Divide total return by the original investment amount.

There's an old adage in the stock market: "Trees can't grow to the sky." This means that a company can only grow so big before it cannot keep growing as quickly as it once did. It can still grow, but the pace will slow. You just can't have 100 percent growth forever. Eventually it becomes mathematically impossible.

To illustrate, if you keep doubling a number, it gets out of hand pretty quickly. Let's dork out for a second. Take a look below at what happens when we double one 25 times:

1, 2, 4, 8, 16, 32, 64, 128, 256, 512, 1024, 2048, 4096, 8192, 16384, 32768, 65536, 131072, 262144, 524288, 1048576, 2097152, 4194304.

If you can earn $1 this year and earn double that amount next year ($2), and earn double that amount next year ($4), and continue that for years and years, you'll be a pretty wealthy person, but it's tough to maintain that pace of 100% growth.

The same goes for company earnings. Eventually, they cannot keep growing as quickly as they once did. Eventually they don't need to keep as much in retained earnings and will return more cash to shareholders in the form of dividends. (You may recall that Earnings = Retained Earnings + Dividends).

Trees don't grow to the sky, they just start paying out cash, and that's OK too. If you go back to the "Money Tree" analogy, you could say in the end the biggest trees usually turn into trees that produce cash too. That cash can be invested in other trees, to make a forest of stocks if you will.

The *direction* of dividends

Just as the direction of earnings matter tremendously, so do the direction of dividends. You can probably tolerate earnings growing slowly if you are being paid a nice amount of cash every quarter. You can probably tolerate it even more if you are getting a pay raise each year. Who likes getting a raise? I do! I do!

That being said, be wary of a dividend that looks too high compared to other stocks. Do your homework to find out *why* the dividend is abnormally high.

Ask yourself questions: Does this stock usually have a dividend this high or did the stock recently drop significantly? A precipitous price drop may be a sign of something seriously wrong even though it makes the dividend yield appear to be large.

Oftentimes when you see this happen, the company has fallen on hard times and investors are anticipating a dividend cut in the future. By the time a company cuts its dividend, the market has usually already figured out that things aren't going well and the stock's price reflects as much for a reason.

You may recall that we've already shown Apple's dividend history. Let's take another look.

Apple Inc. (AAPL)
NasdaqGS - NasdaqGS Real Time Price. Currency in USD

☆ Add to watchlist

157.85 +1.62 (+1.04%)
At close: December 31 4:00PM EST

Buy   Sell

Summary   Chart   Conversations   Statistics   **Historical Data**   Profile   Financials   Analysis   Options   Holders   Sustainability

Time Period: Jan 01, 2015 - Jan 01, 2019 ∨   Show: Dividends Only ∨   Frequency: Daily ∨   Apply

Currency in USD   ⤓ Download Data

Date	Dividends
Nov 08, 2018	0.73 Dividend
Aug 10, 2018	0.73 Dividend
May 11, 2018	0.73 Dividend
Feb 09, 2018	0.63 Dividend
Nov 10, 2017	0.63 Dividend
Aug 10, 2017	0.63 Dividend
May 11, 2017	0.63 Dividend
Feb 09, 2017	0.57 Dividend
Nov 03, 2016	0.57 Dividend
Aug 04, 2016	0.57 Dividend
May 05, 2016	0.57 Dividend
Feb 04, 2016	0.52 Dividend
Nov 05, 2015	0.52 Dividend
Aug 06, 2015	0.52 Dividend
May 07, 2015	0.52 Dividend
Feb 05, 2015	0.47 Dividend

*Close price adjusted for splits.   **Adjusted close price adjusted for both dividends and splits.

All those dividend payments add up over time. Remember, our total return includes both the capital appreciation as well as dividend income. The total of those dividends from 2015 to 2018 totaled $9.54 per share. Recall from earlier that in that same time, from the beginning of 2015 to the end of 2018, the stock price for AAPL went from $111.39 to $157.85. That adds up to capital appreciation of $46.46. Adding $9.54 in dividend income to your return makes a difference:

Capital Appreciation: $157.85 - $111.39 = $46.46

Dividends: $9.54

Total Return: $46.46 + $9.54 = $56.00

To calculate the "total yield" or "percentage return" on your investment, divide your total return by the original investment.

$56.00 total return ÷ $111.39 investment = 50.27%

Fifty percent in four years—that's not a bad investment! It won't make you rich overnight, but remember what we learned about good returns when repeated over "years and years." Let's just say the force of compound interest will be with you.

The PE ratio

Recall our discussion of the PE ratio for both Lemonade Inc. and Apple Inc. from Chapter 9. I showed you businesses of all size often use a multiple of annual earnings to come up with a value of how much the business is worth. Just like two neighbor kids offering us three and four times our annual profits, Apple was going for 13.25 times 2018 earnings. We even discussed how Netflix was selling for 101.5 times 2018 earnings.

With our PE ratio Rosetta Stone, you learn so much about what the market thinks about a company. If Netflix is selling for over 100 years of 2018 earnings, and Apple is selling for 13, who do you think is expected to grow earnings faster? The answer is Netflix. Also, factor in that Apple pays a dividend and Netflix does not.

In this example we are comparing two companies that are not in the same business. We are comparing, dare I say, apples and oranges? It makes them difficult to compare to each other. Apple and Netflix's businesses are unique, so it makes them difficult to compare to any company. Who are their direct competitors? It is more helpful to compare the PE of your company to the PE of other companies that do the same thing. For example, compare Ford to GM, Nike to Under Armour, Coke to Pepsi, Salt to Pepper, Cats to Dogs—you get the point.

You might also find it helpful to compare the PE of your company to "the market". It can be difficult to define what is the market, as there are so many stocks and types of stocks.

To keep us from going down a rabbit hole we won't get out of until you are fast asleep, let's just compare it to the most common definition of the U.S. stock market: the S&P 500 Index.

The S&P 500 Index typically trades for around 13 to 17 times prior year earnings.[1] At extremes, it has traded below 10 and above 20. That tells you that Apple trades for a little cheaper than the market, and Netflix for much more than the market. That doesn't mean you should buy one or the other, but it does add additional color to the story on the stock.

Nerd Word Alerts

Index: A collection of stocks used to help measure various aspects of the market. Used for specific groups of stocks. For example, you will see indexes for small stocks, medium stocks, dividend stocks, oil stocks, tech stocks, etc.

S&P 500 Index: Represents 500 U.S. stocks with market caps above around $5 billion selected by a committee at the company Standard & Poor's. It's *not* the 500 largest companies, it's the 500 chosen by Standard & Poor's. Why do we use it? That's another rabbit hole...

The *direction* of PE

Just as the direction of earnings and the direction of dividends matter tremendously to stock price performance, it is also good to think about the direction of the PE ratio or the multiple.

Given your view of the company's story at this point, do you think the PE will expand or contract going forward? Where has the PE of the stock been historically.

The chart below came from the website ycharts.com, a great place to look at charts and tables of PE ratios over time. Since 2011, Apple's PE has been between 9 and 21 times.

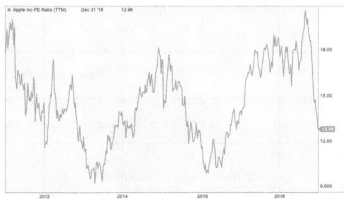

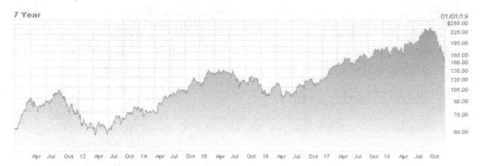

Nerd Word Alert

Multiple Expansion (Contraction): The PE ratio (multiple) decreasing or increasing.

Even if earnings stay the same, you can make money if the PE expands (or lose when it contracts). In the same way, even if the PE stays the same, you can still make money if earnings expand (or lose when they contract).

PE or multiple expansion, earnings stay the same:

> *$1.00 EPS x8 PE = $8.00 stock*
>
> *$1.00 EPS x12 PE = $12.00 stock*

Earnings expansion, PE stays the same:

> *$1.00 EPS x 8 PE = $8.00 stock*
>
> *$1.50 EPS x 8 PE = $12.00stock*

You may recall we received two offers for Lemonade Inc.—one at three times EPS and one at four times EPS. The price of the company went up without us growing earnings. The same is true in the market. Earnings are only reported four times per year, yet the stock prices jump around all over the place, all day long. That's the PE changing each time, just like when we received our two bids on Lemonade Inc.:

> *$60 in earnings x 3 (multiple) = $180 or $90 per share*
>
> *$60 in earnings x 4 (multiple) = $240 or $120 per share*

The Balance Sheet

Don't get too hung up on analyzing a company's balance sheet. It's good info to know, but we aren't in position to be picking apart company balance sheets with kids just yet.

The things you might need to know are "assets" and "liabilities."

Nerd Word Alerts

Balance Sheet: A report or "financial statement" showing a company's equity, assets, and liabilities.

Assets: Something of value owned by the company.

Liabilities: Debts against an individual or company.

Equity: The ownership interest in a business. Equity = Assets - Liabilities

To view a company's balance sheet, pull up a quote. Look for Financials, then Balance Sheet. You may also be able to find other information on debt in Statistics sections. There you will see breakdowns of assets and liabilities.

It can be interesting to see how much cash and debt are on a company balance sheet. It's also interesting to see the direction of the debt and cash. Are either of them building or decreasing at a high rate?

Thoughts on debt

Debt is not a bad thing for a company. Too much debt is a bad thing. That's reasonable. Most companies have debt, and it is way above the paygrade of me and my kids to get in their face about it.

Besides, rarely is debt alone the reason a company goes bankrupt. Bad businesses get into debt problems. Good businesses rarely get into debt problems. Good businesses attract additional investment money before debt becomes a problem, in my experience.

Don't get me wrong, too much debt can slow growth and slow stock price growth. However, if the stock's story is legit enough for you to notice it, and they have earnings to back it up, they can usually deal with debt.

Summarizing the numbers

There are no shortage of numbers and ratios and other things we could cover, but I don't want to cover more than we need. It really can and should be simple to pick good companies for investment.

So far, we've talked about developing the story by watching for good businesses we can understand. We've talked about many of the most important numbers in stock picking: earnings, dividends, the PE ratio, and a little bit about debt. We also talked about the direction of those numbers.

As I will explain, thinking about the direction of those numbers is where the numbers weave into expectations and where the math weaves into psychology.

You probably realize this, but we already talked about many aspects of expectations as we've built this process together.

As we progress through the rest of the book, we'll weave more and more psychology and behavioral finance into the conversation.

Nerd Word Alert

Behavioral Finance: The psychology of economic decision making.

Let's get out of the numbers before they make us weird.

Note

1) "What is the average annual return for the S&P 500?", Investopedia, https://www.investopedia.com/ask/answers/042415/what-average-annual-return-sp-500.asp#ixzz5WD9fI9aA

14 | Stock Picking 375: Expectations

Stocks are all about expectations. The story and numbers we've discussed have expectations built into them. Your frame of mind has expectations build into it. It takes successfully navigating both to be successful as a stock picker. You must find the company you want to buy, but you must also behave properly after you buy it to have long-term success.

This chapter will cover the expectations built into the story and numbers. The next chapter will cover behavior before and after your purchase.

Direction: Predicting the future

In the previous chapter, we discussed the direction of numbers. Direction implies some level of expectation or assumption on what the future will look like. Thinking about the direction of things is where story, numbers, expectations, and psychology come together.

> "It's tough to make predictions, especially about the future." — Yogi Berra

You're predicting the future when you assume earnings will be the same next year, or higher next year—or anything at all next year. Accountants and lawyers gave us the phrase "forward-looking statements," and we're all very thankful.

Nerd Word Alert

Forward-looking Statements: The nerdiest way possible to say "predicting the future."

Remember what we've learned: Stocks follow earnings. Stocks follow dividends. Stocks follow PE ratios. Investors have expectations for the direction of earnings and the direction of dividends and PE ratios. The expectation of the direction of these numbers determines stock price performance. That's a brain twister, but it's the truth.

As an example, companies report earnings quarterly. If a company surpasses the expected earnings numbers, but tells investors future numbers will be weaker than expected, the stock will likely be punished. That's because investors found their expectations about the direction of the numbers was wrong, which influences what they will be willing to pay in PE.

Important: Be aware of your expectations, the expectations of others, and where these expectations may be right or wrong. To over-simplify, when expectations change, stock prices change.

Recency bias

When it comes to our expectations for the future, things that have happened more recently have greater influence on our expectations than things that happened long ago. There is a natural tendency for humans to assume life will continue as it has in the recent past. If a stock has been going up and all the news is good, it's easy to feel like it will keep going up and the news will stay good forever. The same is true when it's going down and all the news is bad.

Story and number expectations

In Chapter 12, we discussed *always be looking around the corner*. I gave you a list of questions to consider with the point being to think about where you see your company over the long-term so you can set your expectations for the future.

We talked about line-out-the-door factor and to consider whether we thought there would be a line in 12 months...or 12 years. This is an example of making sure you understand expectations. What are your expectations of the story?

All the things we know, as well as our expectations regarding those things, are relevant. One change to our expectations for earnings or dividends or PE changes the story. Let me illustrate.

Think about our Netflix example when we discussed PE ratios. Netflix trades at over 100 times earnings because the investors have expectations about the directions of earnings. The share price as of 12/31/2018 was $268 and earnings for the year were $2.66.

The image below is from the Yahoo Finance quote for NFLX, in the Analysis tab. It shows the EPS growth estimates. Notice that over the past five years, NFLX has averaged around 50 percent EPS growth. Analysts are also expecting 50 percent EPS growth *again*. Could that be recency bias? Perhaps.

I'm not trying to sway an opinion, I'm just adding to the story and the expectations for NFLX as an investment.

Growth Estimates	NFLX
Current Qtr.	-10.90%
Next Qtr.	16.50%
Current Year	51.10%
Next Year	63.20%
Next 5 Years (per annum)	49.84%
Past 5 Years (per annum)	48.24%

Let's take a look at what those numbers mean in real life. I like to perform a quick check on what that means for the "out-years."

Nerd Word Alert

Out-years: What EPS and PE look like based on expectations for a few years from now, not just next year and last year.

What if $2.66 grows 50 percent per year for five years? Recall from Chapter 6 that 50% is the same as 0.50, and adding one gets you to the final balance including interest.

It gets us here:

2019 $2.66 x 1.5 = $3.99 EPS

2020 $3.99 x 1.5 = $5.99 EPS

99

> 2021   *$5.99 x 1.5 = $8.98 EPS*
>
> 2022   *$8.98 x 1.5 = $13.47 EPS*
>
> 2023   *$13.47 x 1.5 = $20.20 EPS*

What do you think NFLX stock will be worth in five years? At a PE of 100 times EPS, it would be worth 100 x $20.20 = $2,020 per share in 2023. That gives us an equivalent market cap of about $874 billion. A PE of 50 gives us a stock price of $1,010 and a market cap of $437 billion. A 25 PE gives us $504 and a market cap of $219 billion.

> 2023 PE at EPS of $20.20
>
> 100 x 20.20 = $2,020 per share
>
> 50 x $20.20 = $1,010 per share
>
> 25 x $20.20 = $504 per share

Where could I be wrong or right?

Assume the earnings estimates above come true. It *is* based on the analysis of Wall Street analysts, after all. Well, if they keep growing at 50 percent, they might keep a 100 PE. Netflix has *never* had a low PE ratio or been a "cheap" stock. Since 2013, the PE has ranged between 87 and 420 times earnings.

NFLX doesn't have to keep a 100 PE to be a good stock if they hit their earnings. Assume the PE doesn't hold the 100 level, because that's pretty high compared to the market average at roughly 15 and AAPL at a PE of 13 today. At a PE of 25, we still get to a stock price over $500, almost twice the current price of $268. Obviously $2,020 would be even better!

What if things don't go exactly the way you think they're going to go? (What could go wrong?) What if Amazon, Disney, Apple, Google or others continue to come out with more and more competitive services?

Perhaps all these services are complementary, and Netflix grows at another 50 percent a year for five years. Let's run the numbers with the expectation that they don't.

Running 50 percent EPS growth for two years, then 25 percent EPS growth for three years gets us here:

2019 $2.66 x 1.5 = $3.99 EPS

2020 $3.99 x 1.5 = $5.99 EPS

2021 $5.99 x 1.25 = $7.48 EPS

2022 $7.48 x 1.25 = $9.35 EPS

2023 $9.35 x 1.25 = $11.69 EPS

What should our expectation be for the Netflix PE if this is the path of earnings? Probably not 100 times. Let's try 50 and 25.

$11.69 x 50 = $584 per share

$11.69 x 25 = $292 per share

Compared to the current $268, that's quite a difference in your investment performance.

For comparison sake, I've included the analyst estimates for Apple as well. Notice Apple has grown at about 11.72 percent per year the last five years and is expected to grow about 13 percent per year the next five years.

Growth Estimates	AAPL
Current Qtr.	-12.50%
Next Qtr.	-10.30%
Current Year	-4.10%
Next Year	11.60%
Next 5 Years (per annum)	13.00%
Past 5 Years (per annum)	11.72%

The point in going through this exercise with Netflix is to show you the wide range of possible values for a stock.

Nerd Word Alert

Volatility: Refers to how much a stock price moves up and down.

On average, stocks with higher PE ratios will have larger price swings than stocks with low PE ratios. You cannot be surprised if prices are "volatile" on a stock with a PE of 100. You should expect the price to be volatile. The possible price range we calculated was wide, therefore the risk is higher.

Apple, by comparison, should be expected to be relatively less volatile than Netflix. It has a lower PE and it pays a dividend that has grown nicely. Earnings have been stable but still growing at a nice pace.

Know your stock

Expectations can make all the difference in a lot of things, right? This isn't a stock picking thing. This is a life thing. If you're too pumped up for something, it can be a letdown. If you aren't expecting much, you might be pleasantly surprised.

It's similar to "perspective." Seeing something from a different perspective can certainly change our behavior. Looking from a different angle can give an entirely different point of view.

Every now and then, investors get a little too pumped up, and a stock goes up too much. It hurts when you find you were too optimistic as well, and bought it right before it came back to reality. Sometimes investors don't expect much and are pleasantly surprised. If you expected more than others in the market and bought, it feels good because the stock will go up as expectations change for the better.

The reason the market is always moving is that the expectations are always changing.

Remind yourself what type of business you are buying. Are you buying something new and growing or old and established? It is logical when you're starting a new business to expect your sales to fluctuate a little more than they will in 12 months or 12 years. You may need to remind yourself of these expectations if the stock price goes the wrong way for a little while.

Did you buy something with a high PE ratio? If you did, understand that you are accepting inherently larger fluctuations in price. You should expect "volatility." You are also accepting the risk that if the expectations for earnings are not met, your stock price will likely suffer more than if it had a lower PE ratio.

One More Thing

Remember what we've learned:

Stocks Follow Earnings.

Stocks Follow Dividends.

Stocks Follow PE Ratios.

There is one more very important thing:

Stocks Follow "The Market"

Most of the time, the overall market will be moving your stock as much as anything. When the market is up, you will be up. When the market is down, you will be down. Even if nothing changes with your company, when the overall stock market moves, so does your stock.

From day to day it can be difficult to notice any difference between your stock and the stock market as a whole. Over time, you begin to see the returns diverge between "stocks" and the "stock market."

It can be quite frustrating if you did everything right when it comes to selecting the right company. You may have found the *best company ever* at the *best price ever* only to find yourself losing money on the wrong side of a market sell-off.

That sell-off may have zero impact on your stock's earnings or the value people will eventually put on those earnings over the long term. That doesn't matter. Risk is risk when the bears have the ball. Your stock is going down with everyone else's.

You might as well have your expectations set ahead of time that times like this are not just possible, but probable. It will keep you from freaking out at the wrong time.

If you're invested, it isn't much fun when it's happening, but a clear head and a long-term perspective can turn these events into big-time money makers. If you can, try to take advantage of down markets because you can buy stocks "on sale."

Timing the Market

One of the many lessons the market teaches us over and again is that "you can't time the market." This means you cannot predict the direction the market will move, especially in the short term.

In fact, study after study has shown that most investors earn a much lower rate of return than the stock market due to their behavior. They buy and sell instead of leaving it alone.

Over the short term, predicting the market is like trying to pick traffic lanes during rush hour. Just like you can't predict the curveballs that life throws your way, you cannot time the market. It is therefore best to *plan* for uncertainty, so you aren't surprised. And maybe you can even take advantage of it.

Over longer periods of time, the market tends to move higher more predictably and deliver returns worth sticking around for. The chart below begins in 1918. The grey areas represent recessions. As you can see, most of the time, it's a tough gig being a bear!

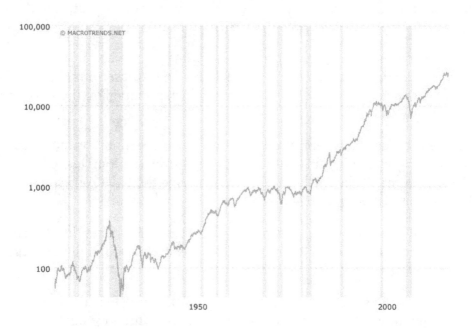

No matter what, you should have expectations that the market will move up and down like a boat captain expecting ocean waves.

Many a fool has lost their way trying to time the market, thinking they could buy and sell quickly to make more money than just picking good companies and holding them for a long time.

I had a professor at The University of Kansas tell us, "You can figure out *what*, but you cannot figure out *when*."

In the late '90s, the internet was new, and investors' imaginations caught fire as the "tech revolution" and "new economy" took hold. My professor was betting *against* the brand-new dot-com stocks that were all the rage. He had been losing money, because he was betting on the market to go down, but it kept going up. Turns out, he wasn't wrong, he was early. Three years early. He got the "what," but he missed on the "when."

In this period, the market saw the stocks of dozens of companies IPO with nothing more than a domain name and a website, then shoot higher (and higher and higher). These companies had no profits, and many had no concrete business model to find their way to profits, but the market was believing the story.

Until it didn't. Suddenly the winds changed, and investors started to care about profits and sales, and these once-darling stocks came crashing down. Many went out of business. This time eventually became known as the "Tech Bubble" or the "Tech Wreck."

The Nasdaq index (similar to the S&P 500) was full of dot-com companies and peaked at 5048 on March 9, 2000. It would bottom over two years later on October 10, 2002 at 1163.37. It wouldn't see that level again until April 23, 2015.

Over the long-term, when you buy doesn't matter as much as what you buy. Good ideas will make you money and bad ideas will lose you money. That's true in any market if you wait long enough. Make sure your *what* is a good long-term business, and then the *when* matters less.

Stock Charts

I waited until the chapter on expectations to discuss the stock chart. It could have been included in Chapter 13 Numbers, but I think it's better served here. The chart is an incredibly useful tool to help give *perspective* on a stock's price.

Reading left to right, stock charts graph the historical price movement of a stock, giving you quite a bit of information in one picture. Most of us are visual learners on at least some level. Looking at a chart can help us better remember historical performance.

Notice you can change multiple settings including the date range. I highly recommend looking at multiple time frames: one-year, three-year, five-year, etc.

You can adjust charts to show a variety of information and they can appear complicated. (What in the heck are all those lines and numbers?) To explain *all* the numbers and lines would leave you begging for mercy, so I'll stick to the most important stuff.

At the end of the previous section, we discussed how stocks follow the stock market. Now is a good time to remind you to also look at charts of the market as a whole (S&P 500 or another index). Most stock quote websites will allow you to overlay your stock chart with a line showing an index for comparison. Doing this helps you understand when the stock is moving because of company performance, and when the stock is just moving because the market is moving.

Nerd Word Alert

Range: The high and low price for a time frame.

Reasons to look at charts:

- Shows the history of the stock price.
- Gives perspective on where we are today relative to the stock's history. Is it high or low?
- Enables you to test your risk tolerance by visualizing yourself investing at different points in time. How much would you have lost or made from point to point?
- Helps you understand how volatile your stock has been historically. What has been the range each year?
- Allows you to see when your stock is moving compared to the rest of the market.

Think about the chart

Look at where the stock has been lately. Where was it priced six, 12, 24 or more months ago? Are you buying a $20 stock that was $10 six months ago? Are you buying a stock that just doubled or tripled in value in the last six months? That might influence your expectations for how volatile the next six months might be. If the stock just had a big run, there should be expectations that I could see that price come down without anything changing in the story.

Imagine buying 100 shares at various points on the chart, and ask how much money you would have at that time? What would you do in each of those different scenarios?

If I bought 100 shares of The Stucco Bathtub Company at $10 per share and watched it go to $5 per share, that means my $1,000 just turned into $500. Could I live with that? What if my $10,000 turned to $5,000? The rate of return was the same in each of those examples, but one hurt quite a bit more than the other.

If the price is lower, see if you can figure out why. If it's a good company with a business you believe in, you may want to take advantage of the lower price to buy shares. Just make sure the story is still intact if the stock is down.

If the stock is at all-time highs, that doesn't mean you need to avoid it. Good stocks tend to lead the market. You may just want to take it a little slower and buy a little now and a little later if it's close to the top.

You don't want to spend so much time looking at the chart that it prevents you from doing anything. A good stock may never get to that low point on the chart again, so don't count on it doing so and then never buying. More on "when to buy" in the next chapter.

All this information adds to story, numbers, and expectations. I find the stock chart helps keep me stay grounded to the story and numbers better than without it.

Trading vs. Investing

As we discuss both expectations and charts, it's a perfect time to distinguish between a "trader" and an "investor." Typically, a trader is someone that will move in and out of a stock quickly, only owning it for minutes, days or weeks at a time, hoping to score a quick profit. An investor is someone interested in making a longer-term commitment based on the prospects of the business.

Both could be considered gambling their money, as both are running the risk of losing it in hopes of making more than they would by putting it into something safer. But investing is more akin to starting a business, while trading is more akin to gambling. One implies a much higher ratio of success to failure than the other.

This is important to understand: There are millions and millions of successful long-term investors in the world, and all they did was keep it extraordinarily simple. They had no special training. In the same vein, very few people have been successful short-term traders for long periods of time. I'm not saying they don't exist, but the few that have been successful developed highly specialized skills and strategies.

This book teaches you to think like a long-term investor.

I bring this discussion up in the section on stock charts because there is debate among nerds in the financial world on the relative importance of charts in the decision-making process.

Nerd Word Alerts

Fundamental analysis: Considering the business prospects and financial health of a company to form an opinion on a stock. The process in this book uses fundamental analysis.

Technical analysis: The science of charting stocks.

Investors typically care more about "fundamentals" of a company and traders typically care more about what they see in the stock chart or the "technicals." In fact, many traders care *only* about the stock chart.

In my opinion, charts are an important tool, but they aren't the only tool.

Fundamental investors are smart to use charts as a tool to help them develop their perspective, but in the end, they aren't buying a stock because of the chart, they're buying it for the business.

Discipline

Expectations can have enormous influence over our behavior regarding when we buy and sell stocks. If we expect our stock to drop, how can we be surprised if it happens? If we know we need to focus on long-term performance, we should probably focus on long-term performance.

We want to be in a disciplined frame of mind to prevent making emotional decisions. Unlike charts and PE ratios, emotions are not helpful tools for investors.

Discipline means:

> *Ground yourself in the story and numbers.*
>
> *Expect the stock and the market to go down.*
>
> *Don't freak out, man. Keep your emotions in check.*

In the next chapter we will dig deeper into the importance of discipline in deciding whether to buy, hold or sell a stock.

15 | Stock Picking 425: Buy, Hold or Sell?

Using the process

I can't tell you that the kids and I pored over the earnings history of each company on our list like analysts, because we didn't. By the time my kids were picking their real money stocks, they were ages 8, 9, and 10.

Let's go back to where we started in the stock picking process, talking about "watching" for businesses as you walk through life. That's what we did.

We looked at each potential stock to check if the company was making money and we checked the PE ratio and the dividend. Then we narrowed the list, picked our favorites, and pulled the trigger. We didn't overthink it by any means.

As the kids get older and show more interest, the conversations get deeper into the process.

In the years leading up to that point, we talked about good businesses we saw; we looked for a good story. We Googled whether they were publicly traded or not. We got into the numbers a little to see if they were profitable and to set our expectations correctly. Then we bought.

They had $500 each to work with, so we limited it to one or two stocks. For their first purchases, Annabel bought Disney (DIS), Henry bought Apple (AAPL), and Max bought both.

Then they didn't freak out. They didn't freak out because they set their expectations correctly.

Remember the process: Story, Numbers, Expectations.

- What's the story? What makes you want to own this business?
- What are the numbers? How much money are they making?
- What should our expectations be for the company and stock?

It is simple to know, but easy to forget that stocks represent real people and real businesses trying to make it in the world.

Keep this in mind and you'll find yourself on the road to investment success.

When to buy

My kids just naturally wanted to buy stocks at lower prices. Who could blame them? We all do. In reality, they bought when they had the money. They didn't try to time the market. In my experience, waiting for cheaper prices generally means you'll see higher prices.

I've seen perfectly rational and intelligent adults (OK fine, it was me) tend to panic when a stock starts to move down while they are waiting to buy. It's easy to change your mind and not pull the trigger, only to watch it bounce higher than when you started watching the stock.

When is the right time to buy? The right answer is usually right now, when you have the money. Good ideas don't stay cheap forever. Don't forgo dollars trying to save dimes by waiting for the absolute bottom and never investing. While you're waiting for your stock to go "just a few cents lower," it might end up a few *dollars* higher.

No big bets

All investors make mistakes and lose money, even the best investors in the world. It's part of the game. The best investors stay in the game because they never put themselves in a situation where one bad bet can take them out of the game. All of us need to follow the same logic. Greed can pull you to make big bets – don't let it happen.

If you expect your stock to be volatile or risky, don't make a big bet. To stay out of trouble, consider following the rule of "smaller bets for larger risks". Your psychology plays a vital role in your success or failure as an investor. Making smaller investments can help protect that psychology from doing the wrong thing at the wrong time.

Be systematic

If you're teaching a child to invest in stocks or other assets, hopefully this is something they do for a lifetime. That's how you build wealth. If you plan to make continuous contributions to the account, then all the more reason to avoid spending too much time analyzing when to buy. With systematic or regular contributions, you'll naturally gain the advantage of dollar-cost averaging.

Nerd Word Alert

Dollar-cost Averaging: A strategy of investing an *equal dollar amount* on a schedule over time so you are naturally purchasing more shares when markets are low and fewer shares when markets are high. The investor would plan to buy $Xoo dollars in stock every week or month for X weeks or months.

Look for sales

If you really want to know the best time to buy, it's when everything looks the bleakest. When everyone is selling, and the market is dropping. It may not feel like it at the time, but you might be glad you did after a few months or years.

> "Be fearful when others are greedy and greedy when others are fearful." –Warren Buffett

The market goes down from time to time, and when it happens it drags all companies down, not just the bad ones. If you're invested, it isn't much fun when it's happening, but a clear head and a long-term perspective can turn these events into big-time money makers. If you can, try to take advantage of down markets because you can buy stocks "on sale."

It's much easier to buy low and sell high if you have cash on hand when the stock market "sells off" and prices are low. You can't take advantage if you haven't prepared for it. That's why it's important to keep a cash reserve as discussed in Chapter 7.

In March 2009, the S&P 500 hit its low point after the 2008 crash. Nine years later it was up 298 percent from that bottom. The investors that stepped in when fear was at its peak made a *lot* of money.

I'm a fan of looking at stock charts for this very reason. Looking at a long-term chart of the market or a stock shows you how much money you would have made by being a buyer in the last bear market. Looking at the charts over and over helps reinforce to you the right behavior in

113

the *next* bear market. Next time BE A BUYER!

Shelby Davis, founder of Davis Selected Advisers, manages about $100 billion in several investment funds and has a good quote for us here:

> "You make most of your money in a bear market, you just don't realize it at the time."

Aside from whole market downturns when all stocks go on sale, company or industry specific issues will put individual stocks on sale as well. It can be another great time to pick up a stock at a discount, but don't get caught buying just because it's cheap if the story is deteriorating. On the other hand, if you feel the stock is only in a temporary dog house, then you might be getting a good deal on a good company. More Warren Buffett wisdom on this situation:

> "The best thing that happens to us is when a great company gets into temporary trouble. We want to buy them when they're on the operating table."

The Psychology of Gains and Losses

Nobody likes losing money. Nobody. Everybody likes making money. Everybody.

For most people, there are two certainties: death and taxes. For investors, there are three certainties: death, taxes, and losses.

If you're investing in stocks, you *will* inevitably lose money at one point or another. It's almost a rite of passage for your first stock to drop immediately after you buy it. You might as well get it over with.

So, what's an investor to do when their stock drops?

Don't freak out, man

Most of your success in investing depends not on the quality of the investment, but on your behavior as an investor. You must train yourself to react without emotion in the face of things that trigger an emotional response.

It can be extraordinarily stressful when money is on the line. With time and experience, the feelings won't affect you as much. You'll get used to the process and your brain will remember that it didn't kill you last time.

Just as we don't naturally want to run into dangerous situations, proper training can enable us to act calmly in the face of danger or stressful situations.

Think about all the things people do that would make an untrained person freak out. First responders do it every day. Soldiers do it every day. Medical professionals. Extreme athletes. Proper training can enable us to do pretty extraordinary things in intense environments.

Proper training can make us better investors as well. The common denominator in training for all these activities is learning to control our natural fight-or-flight adrenaline response, also called "acute stress syndrome." Then we can use our thinking brain, not our emotional, animal brain. You might not be able to stop the feelings—it's a physiological, chemical response in your brain and body. But you can be aware and prepared for the feelings, so you don't let them control your behavior.

Kids may be better suited for investing than grown-ups, because they are actually better at taking the emotion out of it. Grown-ups are more emotional about money. Why? WE MIGHT NEED THAT MONEY SOME DAY!

Kids forget about the money conversation the minute they leave the room. Plus, parents pay the bills. Who needs money? Even when you thought they were listening to your money talk, they were really thinking about Fortnite.

It may sound simple, but take the advice of the psychologists at thebodysoulconnection.com. If you're really having a hard time dealing with stress over your investments, do what you make your kids do when they break down. Take a time out.

Stop thinking about your investments. Breath. Exercise. Do Yoga. Slowing your breathing slows your mind's response and calms the "act now" response.

Do whatever you have to do to chill out, then see if you can find where you left your brain. Investing is a thinking person's game. There's no crying in stocks.

When your stock drops

It's very tempting to sell when your investments are down. It's human nature. Selling will ease the pain and you'll feel better for a while, but you won't make any money selling low. Sure, you might be able to dodge some additional downside and in theory buy lower, but it just doesn't happen. I've heard so many people tell me "I'll get out now and buy lower later," but they *never buy lower*!

Here's why. If you are already looking to sell when you're down, you're scared on some level. You're scared to lose your money and never get it back. The fear level is elevated, right?

You say you're going to buy back lower? For things to get even lower than they already are, things will have to get even scarier. The fear level will need to rise from its already heightened state.

What makes you think you're going to be "not scared" enough to confidently step in when things get even worse? You'll more likely say "see I told you it was going to get worse" and think you're a genius for not losing more money. (Notice you didn't make anything—you just didn't keep losing.)

When will you step back in? "When things settle down…" is the typical response. So, when things get *less scary*? When the fear level is lower?

What you're saying is that you'll buy back when prices are higher? Because when things are scary, prices go down. When things "settle down," prices go up.

You will hear this again from me because it's so important: The market looks *forward*, and it looks forward and around corners much quicker than any of us, let alone non-professional investors.

If you're someone who sells when things are scary and down, you aren't the type of person who will buy lower. You aren't the "run into a burning building" type when it comes to the stock market. You will buy higher when things have settled down.

You'll be better off keeping a long-term perspective and riding out the downside, or better yet, having your eggs in different baskets. Remember, it's good to have different types of money trees in your garden in case one type of tree has a bad season.

That's Henry (age 7) above, hiking across Catalina Island, trying to focus on the long-term goal instead of the short-term pain.

What's changed besides the stock price?

You want to ask yourself what has changed besides the stock price? There's a reason you bought the stock. It had a story, it had numbers, and you had expectations.

Has anything changed?

If you answer yes, you may need to reassess. Go back through the process beginning in Chapter 12.

> "When the facts change, I change my mind, what do you do sir?"
> –John Maynard Keynes

It is reasonable to change your mind if the facts have changed sufficiently. Don't let your pride keep you in a dog of a stock.

Decide how serious an issue it *really* is. Make sure you aren't making a knee-jerk reaction. Rerun the numbers. If the company had one bad quarter, does that really break the long-term story?

Or is the stock price the only thing that's really changed? Then you probably don't have to do anything at all. Isn't this what you expected?

You can try to figure out why the stock price has changed. Is there company or industry specific news driving the move? Is the market moving? Remember we discussed that "stocks follow the market" more often than not.

Don't throw good money after bad

If you bought a stock you liked at $20, and it drops to $15 with no changes to the story, you should *love* it at $15, right? Well maybe, but maybe not.

Once again, we must start with your expectations going into the investment. If your plan was to buy half the investment, then wait and add to it later if it pulled back, then stick to your plan. That's an unemotional plan based on logic and realistic expectations.

If you already put as much into the investment as you want, but now are trying to "double down" to get it back, that's dangerous behavior, driven by emotion.

> "The most important thing to do if you find yourself in a hole is to stop digging." –Warren Buffett

Bulls and Bears

Remember again that "stocks follow the market." The market is almost freaking out all the time. On average, the entire market pulls back (drops) about ten percent once per year. It's called a correction because usually it occurs when stocks have overshot reasonable levels and need to correct. When this occurs, individual stocks can easily pull back more than the market.

A bear market, defined as a market pulling back 20 percent or more for longer than two months, can be more painful.

If you watch CNBC for a day, you'll think bear markets happen all the time. There is never a shortage of "experts" on TV predicting one. In reality, we've had eight since 1926. EIGHT. In 92 years.

The average bear market has lasted 1.4 years with an average loss of 41%. Ouch. If the entire market is down that much, you know many stocks are down much more.

The good news is that the average bull market has lasted 9.1 years with an average return of 473 percent.

It pays to be bullish. History[1] is certainly on your side.

Earnings season

In the U.S., publicly-traded companies report earnings quarterly or four times per year. A good chunk of them report in a four- to six-week cluster each quarter called "earnings season." You get quite a lot of company information in those four to six weeks.

The reason it matters is that earnings move the market and they move the stocks of the companies reporting them. If lots of stocks report good earnings, then the whole market tends to perform well. If the opposite is true, then stocks will probably go down. Stocks follow earnings, right?

Your stock may also react to earnings reports from its competitors or suppliers, or even its customers. Maybe your stock is down because one of its competitor's had a bad earnings report and everyone thinks the whole industry is bad. Maybe the whole industry isn't bad, that competitor was doing poorly because your company is taking its customers! How silly would you feel if you panic-sold your stock only to watch it rocket higher days later on good earnings?

Between earnings seasons, you wait without much company information, but there's always plenty of non-company news to move the markets. The market gets pushed around by political stories, random upgrades and downgrades from analysts you've never heard of, etc. Most of these stories don't matter one bit to your company, but the stock price may move down anyway.

Here's a tip: Don't get shaken out of your great stock because the stock market is worried about democrats and republicans not getting along. Here's a prediction: they're not going to get along. Expect it.

When it goes up

What do we do when the stock goes up and we have a profit? Hopefully you get to ask yourself this question often.

> "When we own portions of outstanding businesses with outstanding managements, our favorite holding period is forever." –Warren Buffett

If you sell for gains too quickly or frequently, it can have unintended consequences to your portfolio.

We may have a tendency to "trim our flowers and plant our weeds." We sell our good ideas too early to lock in gains and we dig in and defend our dogs for too long. If you sell your winners and keep your losers, you end up with a portfolio of losers.

Just as we did with stock drops, we should go back through the process. Where are we in the story, numbers and expectations? If you expect changes, then re-assess.

One thing I've learned in my lifetime of investing, is that doing *all* of any one thing is almost always wrong over the long term. Taking profit too often is not a good idea, and neither is never taking a profit.

Bernard Baruch, economic advisor to U.S. Presidents Woodrow Wilson and Franklin D. Roosevelt, said it this way:

> "Nobody ever lost money taking a profit."

Another old Wall Street adage is, "Bulls make money. Bears make money. Pigs get slaughtered." This is an ever so clever way of saying "don't get greedy."

Sell half

> "When you reach the fork in the road, take it."
> —Yogi Berra

When I'm really torn between what to do, I sell half. You'll feel a little bit smart and a little bit dumb, no matter what happens.

If the stock drops, you'll say "Yay, I sold half." But if it moves higher, "Yay, I kept half."

Note

1) History of Bear and Bull Markets Since 1926, First Trust Portfolios LP, 2018, https://www.ftportfolios.com/Common/ContentFileLoader.aspx?ContentGUID=4ecfa978-d0bb-4924-92c8-628ff9bfe12d

16 | Mutual Funds and ETFs

For most Americans, their initial and perhaps only exposure to investing in the bond or stock market is through mutual funds or exchange-traded funds, two classic investment nerd words.

> **Nerd Word Alert**
>
> **Mutual Fund**: A way to invest in many stocks and/or bonds at once. Your investment is pooled with other investors, and the management company purchases the shares on your behalf. One share of a fund may represent dozens to hundreds of investments inside it. Shares only trade once a day, at the close of the market.
>
> **Exchange Traded Fund (ETF)**: Similar to a mutual fund, but shares can be traded throughout the day.

Both mutual funds and ETFs pool investor money to buy tens to hundreds of stocks with one purchase. Most corporate 401(k) and other retirement plans use some type of "fund" for their investments.

Truth be told, my kids would look at you like a deer in headlights if you asked them what a mutual fund or ETF is. The irony is that I worked for a mutual fund company for most of their lives. (They just knew I worked in the stock and bond business). It's important for us to cover the basics of these two investment options, since they are the most mainstream method of investing in the stock and bond markets.

With mutual funds and ETFs, your investment is spread over many different companies. Instead of owning the stocks and bonds directly, you own shares of the fund. The fund management company decides which stocks and/or bonds to buy and sell.

There are benefits to buying funds instead of picking stocks.

For one, you don't have to decide when or what to buy and sell. The fund managers do that for you. That being said, there are a larger number of different funds to choose from than there are different stocks.

Another benefit is instant diversification. You can spread your risk if you own one or more funds rather than just one or two stocks.

Another way to think about mutual funds and ETFs, is to think of two large windows on a house. One window is divided into several smaller panes of glass, and the other is made from one large pane. If the neighbor kid throws a baseball at your house, which window could be more damaged? If he hits the single-pane window, you're replacing the entire window. If he hits the other window, it's just one small pane that must be fixed.

Mutual funds and ETFs are the window divided into small panes. Because the fund owns many different stocks or bonds, if one company falls on hard times, it won't destroy your entire investment.

Funds also give you the ability to buy certain parts of the market or certain strategies. For example, you could buy a fund focused on just oil stocks, or just bank stocks.

There are benefits, but there are also costs associated with funds. Each fund has management and other expenses that come out of your profits. Also, just as each company has its own story, numbers, and expectations, so does each fund.

Nerd Word Alerts

Active Fund: Mutual fund or ETF designed to beat the return of a particular market or index.

Passive Fund: Mutual fund or ETF designed to match the return of a particular market or index.

Active strategies usually have higher expenses than passive strategies. You tend to see more passive strategies in the ETF world versus the mutual fund world, but both fund types offer both strategies.

If you buy an active strategy, make sure you do your research and don't chase short-term performance. Look at long-term (10 years or more) track records and try to understand what particular index the fund is comparing itself to. Just like with stocks, you need to know what you own.

Individual stocks vs. funds

There is debate regarding owning stocks and bonds individually versus owning funds. The less experience and comfort you have investing for yourself, the more you should seek advice from professionals. Interview several advisors, ask lots of questions, and seek referrals from people you know and trust.

Regardless of your experience level, teaching (yourself and) your kids the process of buying individual stocks will make them better at more than just buying stocks. It will take them into the mind of the business owner and capitalist.

Kids (and adults) are likely to be more engaged in the process with individual stocks than with mutual funds or ETFs. It's more tangible and exciting to think about an individual company story than a fund story. Even if the bulk of your investments are in mutual funds and ETFs, you still probably check on the individual stocks you own more frequently.

There is value in trying to pick winners. Even if you don't win or beat the market—or whatever you are trying to do with that investment—you gain value in going through the process. If you do good research and make well thought-out investment decisions, you will learn from paying attention to the outcomes. You'll recognize what went right and wrong, and get better at it. You might not win on this one, but maybe you learn what you need to win on the next one.

What's that Edison quote about failure? There are a bunch of them, but here's one I've heard before:

> "I have not failed. I have just found 10,000 ways that won't work."

Hopefully you don't need 10,000 misses to have a winner.

> "Failure is the road to success."

That's better!

Or how about one from motivational speaker and author Denis Waitley:

> "Failure should be our teacher, not our undertaker."

17 | History: Lessons Learned From Business Successes...and Failures

There is absolutely no substitute for experience. I'm going to try to help you skip steps on the investment learning curve by sharing a few investment stories. A few of these stories come from conversations with the kids and a few from my experiences in general.

While these stories are stocks that have already performed, we can learn from their history.

> "What we learn from history is that people don't learn from history." –Warren Buffett

Choosing stocks with kids

When the kids bought stock, we talked about quite a few names. Some of those names ended up in their portfolio, and some ended up in their "game" portfolio (recall Chapter 3). Most never ended up anywhere.

As the kids had ideas, I often used my "professional judgement" to lead them towards "blue chips." I was worried about nerd stuff like earnings per share and PE ratios. Oftentimes you make more money buying what you *see* instead of what you *study*.

Nerd Word Alert

Blue Chips: Well-known, well-established, larger companies that have established track records.

Netflix vs. Disney

Disney has been a profitable company for a long time, much longer than any of my kids (or maybe even I) have been alive. They pay a cash dividend each quarter and have grown both it and their earnings nicely for years and years.

Netflix, at the time we were looking at our initial list of candidates, was not as profitable as Disney. They were focused on growing their business very rapidly, and had recently undergone a couple of choppy transitions that swung the stock price up and down.

Since the time we were considering the investment, Netflix has not only become much more profitable, they have disrupted television and movies similar to how Amazon has disrupted retail shopping. (Amazingly, Amazon also competes with Netflix in streaming television and movies.)

I steered my daughter toward purchasing Disney instead of Netflix using my "professional" judgement. Since then, we've seen what a great growth story Netflix has become, growing six times faster than Disney as shown in the five-year chart below from Nasdaq.com. (NFLX is darker line, DIS lighter line.)

Netflix vs. Disney

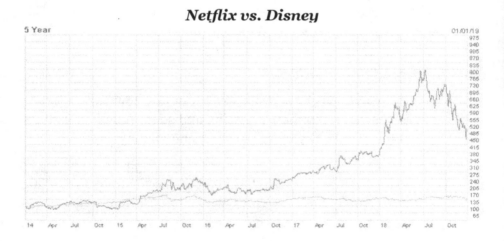

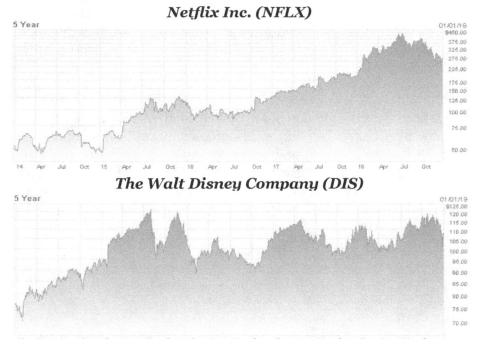

Always be looking around the corner

To give myself some credit, there are also times that general "adulting" can help (maybe) keep kids from buying into a fad instead of a long-term trend. I remember we also talked about Candy Crush and parent King.com LTD. That would *not* have been a good choice. It was a recent IPO and was losing money, and they didn't have another game coming. It turned out to be a dog of a stock and they were later acquired by Activision Blizzard.

As you've heard me mention before, you have to be looking around the corner with investing. What happens *after* what's happening now?

The GoPro story is another example of a stock I may have helped the kids avoid to their benefit. It also was a recent IPO and wasn't making much money. We wondered if people really were going to keep wanting to video themselves doing average things forever. We lived in a very GoPro-heavy town in Southern California, and it seemed everyone who wanted one had one. We knew ours was never charged and we never used it anymore. Good call, as the stock was pretty doggish after a promising IPO.

Similarly, we discussed Fitbit, since mom loved hers. We also saw her lose two of them in a couple months and eventually, not replace it. Also, there were lots of competitors entering the market including Apple. Good call there too!

My kids and I also talked about Target and Wal Mart and how they were under pressure from another stock we looked at—Amazon. We knew we didn't want either retailer, but we also missed by not buying Amazon. At the time, it wasn't very profitable, but was building a massive enterprise with multiple disruptive businesses. As we all know, it has since become quite profitable and continues to grow both the businesses and profits in a meaningful way.

GoPro Inc.

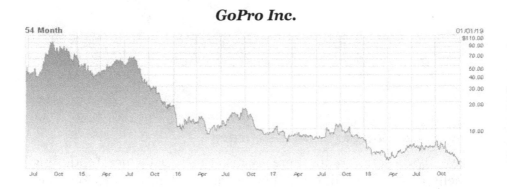

Fitbit Inc.

Amazon.com Inc.

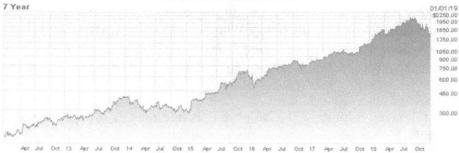

Walmart

Target Corporation

Nintendo

Here's an example from working with my kids and Nintendo stock. We never bought the stock, but we certainly talked about it and the company over the course of a couple years. In the end, it was a missed opportunity, but also a great learning experience.

When "Pokémon Go" arrived on the scenes, it was a whirlwind of a fad. The augmented-reality video game began to really get popular on a Friday leading into a weekend, and by Sunday night it was viral. To those who didn't know any better, it looked like some sort of smartphone zombie apocalypse. Players were following directions on their phones to find and capture virtual Pokémon in parks and public spaces across the map.

The following Monday, the stock for Pokémon Go owner Nintendo rocketed higher on the backs of the phenomenon.

The kids and I talked about the whole crazy thing, including what we thought of it from a stock perspective. We all agreed that "it's a fad that will peak" and wondered how they would make money on it.

You can see the spike in price and volume around July of 2016 in the chart from NASDAQ below. That spike in the stock quickly turned the other way. The chart shows that investors who were buying during that spike had to wait nearly a year before the stock was solidly back to their purchase price, much less making money.

Nintendo Company Limited

In 2017, Nintendo came out with a new handheld console called "Switch." I asked the kids if this was going to be cool. Would kids buy it? Will this be a hit or a dud for Nintendo? They all agreed it would be a big hit. I'm not sure why we didn't buy Nintendo then, but we should have.

Look back at the chart above and you can see a substantial gain starting in early 2017, as Nintendo stock performed on the back of Switch sales. The Switch turned out to be a hit product for Nintendo and a good money maker for both the company and investors.

Line out the door stocks

Starbucks

In the 1990s and early 2000s Americans discovered they had been drinking crappy coffee for generations. They also rediscovered what they already knew; it felt good to get out of the house to catch up with old friends over a beverage.

Howard Schultz knew this when he joined Starbucks in 1981. You didn't need to know it that early to make money from this stock. You only needed to notice a line out the door at the Starbucks whenever one opened in your neighborhood or near your office, and probably a dozen points in between. Unless you live in rural parts of the country, you likely witnessed the Starbucks phenomenon. And you didn't need to be a genius to recognize that business was good at Starbucks.

Not only was there a line out the door, but they were also selling a product with a repeating purchase cycle. For many people, Starbucks was becoming part of their daily routine. That's good business. Coffee is a stimulant and addictive. That's also good for business.

Prior to Starbucks, coffee had become a commodity with very little differentiation between competitors. Starbucks helped evolve the American taste palate, showing the coffee drinkers among us that there were different flavors in the same way there are differences in wine flavors.

Laptop computers, the internet and the "mobile office" were just beginning to become mainstream too. Those mobile office types needed a place to hang out and use (and charge) their laptop. Starbucks was in the perfect place to take full advantage. Where else do you go if you have three hours to kill and need to plug in? The public library might have been your only option until Starbucks.

To give you an example of the gap in the market before Starbucks, I remember being 16 in Wichita, needing a place to fill out job applications for a couple hours. I didn't know where to go. If I had thought of it, I would have gone to the library, but I didn't. Where did I go? Denny's. The coffee sucked and the waitress was pretty annoyed at me for sitting there for an hour without eating.

Starbucks filled several gaps in the market with their high-quality coffee and their hip atmosphere. You didn't need to know that to make money. You only needed to see the line out the door.

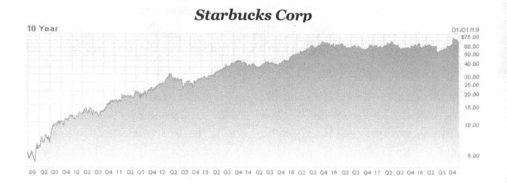

Starbucks Corp

Chipotle

If you live in certain parts of the U.S., you take the local taqueria for granted. You assume the entire world has access to giant burritos filled with home-sized cuts of fresh veggies, salsas, and meats in a "waiter and waitress free" environment.

Even if you DO live in the "taqueria belt," you might find comfort in a national brand. Though the best burritos I've ever had come from the sketchiest burrito stands, I went because I had a friend refer me. Who wants to be the guinea pig to see which hole in the wall taqueria is a diamond in the rough and which one is a pain in the gut?

In most of the country, your options for Mexican food (BTW—the most quickly growing demographic in the U.S. and also one of the most quickly growing food trends of the '90s) were a sit-down restaurant or a fast-food establishment à la Taco Bell. There was no in-between.

Chipotle Mexican Grill capitalized on this gap in the market to begin selling on a national scale those same burritos many of us take for granted.

Even if you didn't recognize the gap between the supply and demand for burritos, you may have noticed the same line-out-the-door indicator as Starbucks. There was almost always a line, and it was usually out the door, from when they opened at 11 a.m. until they closed at 10 p.m.

They also were in tune with a consumer that was becoming more health conscious. As they grew, they were one of the first national chains to use hormone-free ingredients and continuously communicated that they cared about what they put in the food. Their efforts were able to help convince consumers to keep forming lines out the door for years.

Then in 2015, the line was no more. Several food-borne illness outbreaks traced to Chipotle chased customers away.

If there is a line, do a little research. If there used to be a line, and now there isn't, hopefully you sold early.

Chipotle Mexican Grill Inc.

Southwest Airlines vs. United Airlines

Now we know lines can be good. But they also can be bad. Let's use two airlines as an example.

In my career, I've flown millions of domestic miles, mostly in the Western U.S. I've waited in my share of airport lines. When I started travelling, Southwest and United were my primary airlines. In this environment, I observed interesting customer patterns at every airport.

During the financial crisis of 2008, the economy screeched to a halt. Businesses were bracing themselves for not just a run-of-the-mill recession, but for the worst recession they could imagine.

Business travel was an easy target for cost savings. Moratoriums were put on travel and most of the other road warriors were grounded.

There were empty counters almost everywhere. Flights would be full, but there weren't as many, with airlines cutting routes due to the recession.

Except for Southwest. They had the line-out-the-door (and around the building) at every airport I went to. It could be 4:30 a.m. at LAX and they had to snake their check-in line on the sidewalk so it wouldn't overflow into another airline's waiting area.

That was not the case at United or any other airline. There was no line out the door anywhere else.

That was clue No. 1 that Southwest might have a business that is a *lot* better than the others.

My first year on the road, I ended up gravitating towards United because they offered complimentary upgrades to first class once you hit a status level. That's a nice perk, especially on long and overnight flights after working all week on the road. Southwest has one class—coach. I guess I'm a sucker for creature comforts and I ended up sticking with United... for a while.

Flying United avoided that long line out the door at the ticket counter, and then I usually got upgraded because of the lack of travelers.

That didn't save me from long lines. Far too frequently, I found myself in a line of unhappy customers waiting to have a flight re-booked because of issues with my original flight. Regularly missing family and business activities due to delayed United flights began to wear thin.

To add insult to injury, the United customer service agents didn't seem to care much. They were frequently unfriendly and showed little empathy. They certainly weren't going the extra mile to make up for the inconvenience. They seemed to like United about as little as I was beginning to like United. They didn't like to fly, and it showed.

Anyone who travels more than a few times knows that things go wrong. Delays happen. The difference was that when I found myself in the same situation at Southwest, the agents seemed to care. They would try to help get me home another way. They would hold flights if they had transfers. If they couldn't fix it, they said they were sorry. I think they even meant it! They would give me free drink coupons and then never collect them on the plane, so I always had plenty.

That's not what happened at United. I finally had had enough, and vowed my allegiance to Southwest. I ended up giving up my first-class upgrades to fly a million miles a year in coach. To this day, I am *extremely loyal* to Southwest and won't fly United.

Seven years later, it was not terribly surprising to see the viral video of the doctor being dragged from the airplane by his feet with his teeth knocked out. As much as I didn't enjoy seeing that doctor get hurt, there was definite schadenfreude seeing United backpedal as an organization.

So, what does that mean as an investor?

The following shows a comparison of LUV versus UAL from 2012 to 2018. While the spread between the two diminished more recently, you can see substantial outperformance by LUV stock for several years.

LUV vs. UAL

Southwest Airlines Co

United Continental Holdings Inc

FAANG

This acronym was coined by CNBC host Jim Cramer (and then borrowed by *everyone*) to describe a handful of tech stocks that were leading the market for several years in a row. In many ways, the stories of these companies (and stocks) fed off the same theme: mobile connectivity in the first decade of the smartphone.

I'm using them as examples of "stock secrets" hidden in plain sight. How many of us were regular users of these companies but didn't own the stock?

- **F**acebook (FB)
- **A**mazon (AMZN)
- **A**pple (AAPL)
- **N**etflix (NFLX)
- **G**oogle (now Alphabet)(GOOG)

Facebook

Facebook's much anticipated IPO was in May 2012. By that time, the combination of smartphones and social media had turned much of the public into walking zombies, "liking" pictures of each other's food and kids. You saw big-time line-out-the-door factor, as any line out the door was full of people *liking* that they had something to do while waiting in line.

High traffic on social media sites doesn't necessarily translate to successful stock price performance. Remember, stocks follow earnings. How are you making money on all these people liking your app or website?

There was *no question* that Facebook had created something special at the time of their IPO. It was very highly anticipated for that reason. The

138

question investors were asking was, "How are you going to monetize this?" Likes weren't paying the bills back then. Almost all ad revenue at the time of IPO was coming from website traffic, not from mobile traffic. Consumer traffic was definitely shifting to mobile, but would Facebook be able to monetize on a smartphone as they had on the desktop?

In 2012, Facebook made $0.01 per share in earnings. The year prior to the IPO they had made $0.50 per share. There were plenty of questions, despite the obvious line-out-the-door factor. A price of $38 per share on $0.50 earnings is a P/E multiple of 76. Would you pay 76 years of profits up front to buy a share of Facebook? Oh and, by the way, that was last year, in the next year they basically broke even and made a penny a share.

Facebook raised around $16 billion in the offering, at the time the largest in U.S. history. But unless you have the special connections to get the IPO price, your first shot to buy an IPO is at the open of public trading. That price may be higher or lower depending on the market. The FB IPO price was $38, but it opened trading at $42.05, plus there were numerous market technical glitches. (Personally, I had orders to buy shares that I submitted just after it opened for trading. It was over two hours before I received confirmation of the transaction from my online broker. I've never seen this before or since.)

The price spiked that day to over $45, but would close at just over $38 to end the first day of trading. It wouldn't see those levels again for over a year. The stock bottomed in September 2012 at $17.55 and eventually found its way back to the IPO price by August 2013.

Eventually, Facebook figured out how to monetize the line out the door on the smartphone. They were able to substantially grow their ad revenue over the next several years and it showed up in their earnings. They also made several acquisitions, most notably Instagram in 2012 for $1 billion and WhatsApp in 2014 for $19 billion.

Nerd Word Alert

Acquisition: When one company buys another. It can also be called a "takeover." Oftentimes you'll hear the acquired company referred to as "taken out" by the other company.

When rival social media company Snap had its IPO in March 2017, traffic trends had shifted away from Facebook and towards the new kid. This was especially true for younger users. "Snap is for young people; Facebook is for old people" was the line of the day. What you could have missed was that Facebook was poised to compete with Snap just fine thanks to the acquisition of Instagram a few years earlier. Traffic lost to Snap on Facebook was more than made up for due to growth in traffic on Instagram. The company also got much better at monetizing both Instagram and Facebook.

Nerd Word Alert

Monetizing: Turning business metrics like site traffic, users or "eyeballs" into revenue.

Earnings went from $0.01 in 2012 to an eventual $6.15 in 2017 and $7.57 per share in 2018. The stock eventually went as high as $218.62 in July 2018 before dropping to below $150 by the end of 2018.

Facebook not only had the user traffic, they were also making money on it. Compare the stock chart of social media company Twitter (TWTR) as well as Snap (SNAP) below. Now compare the earnings stream of each.

In the same time as Facebook, Twitter has taken earnings from a loss of $0.06 per share in both 2012 and 2013 to a gain of $0.44 in 2017 and $0.86 per share in 2018. Snap has yet to turn a profit, and their investors have needed the app's virtual smiley faces and bunny ears to help them put on a happy face. You can see that the stock price of all three is reflective of how well they've been able to turn their traffic into dollars.

Facebook (FB)

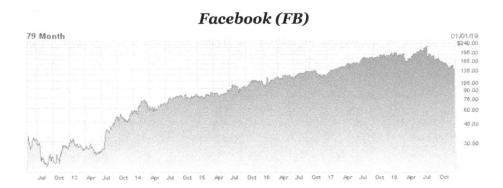

	High/Low Price	EPS
2011		0.50
2012	45/17	0.01
2013	58/22	0.60
2014	82/51	1.10
2015	110/72	1.29
2016	133/89	3.49
2017	184/114	6.15
2018	219/123	7.57

Twitter (TWTR)

	High/Low Price	EPS
2011		-0.12
2012		-0.06
2013	74/17	-0.06
2014	70/29	0.14
2015	53/21	0.40
2016	25/13	0.37
2017	25/14	0.44
2018	47/22	0.86

Snap (SNAP)

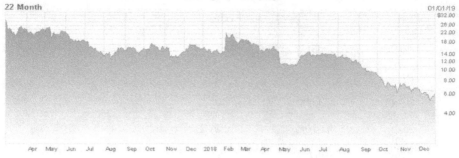

22 Month

01/01/19
$32.00
26.00
22.00
18.00
14.00
12.00
10.00
8.00
6.00
4.00

Apr May Jun Jul Aug Sep Oct Nov Dec 2018 Feb Mar Apr May Jun Jul Aug Sep Oct Nov Dec

	High/Low Price	EPS
2015		-0.32 (Loss)
2016		-0.40
2017	29/11	-0.61
2018	21/4	-0.47

Amazon

Lines out the door matter. We've established that fact. Those lines don't have to be people.

Two lines that showed up in houses across the country could have cued you in on one stock to buy and a *whole bunch* of stocks to avoid. The first line was the line of boxes waiting at the front door from Amazon. It was like Christmas morning for grown-ups five days (then seven days) a week.

If you got home later in the day and missed the first line of boxes, you had another chance to catch this one. The second line was the line of boxes at the recycling bin. If your house was like mine, the bin was full and spilling over. (It's a known fact that only humans over the age of 20 would ever think to break down boxes to make them fit in the bin, by the way.)

Your observation might have led you to not only buy Amazon, but to avoid other stocks that suffered from what Amazon was doing. Many of your traditional retailers saw their businesses suffer as a result of Amazon's growth.

RadioShack, Toys R Us, Sports Authority, and a host of others closed their doors or at least declared bankruptcy and reorganized post 2015. Sears (which acquired an oft-beleaguered Kmart in 2004) has declared bankruptcy as of October 2018 and will be closing hundreds of stores. JC Penney has been on the ropes for years and is hanging on by a thread.

Those companies have been the biggest victims of "The Amazon Effect," but they aren't the only ones. Target (TGT), Walmart (WMT), Macy's (M), Nordstrom (JWN), Best Buy (BBY), and *many* others struggled as Amazon took business.

These stories are still being told, both for Amazon and for all its competitors. But now these companies are fighting back and it will be fun to watch them duke it out. As a consumer, I appreciate being the beneficiary of their competition. I like the trips to the store they've saved me. It gives me more time to break down boxes.

Amazon.com Inc. (AMZN)

	High/Low Price	EPS
2011	246/160	1.37
2012	264/172	0.28
2013	405/242	0.59
2014	408/284	-0.52
2015	696/285	1.25
2016	847/474	4.90
2017	1213/747	4.55
2018	2050/1167	20.14

Walmart (WMT)

	High/Low Price	EPS
2012	77/57	4.57
2013	81/67	5.02
2014	88/72	5.11
2015	90/56	5.06
2016	75/60	4.59
2017	100/65	4.32
2018	109/81	4.42

Target Corporation (TGT)

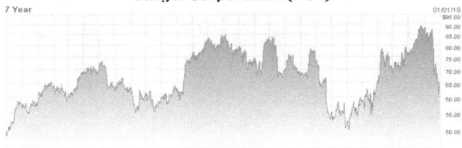

	High/Low Price	EPS
2012	65/47	4.28
2013	73/58	4.37

2014	76/54	4.38
2015	85/68	4.21
2016	84/65	4.69
2017	74/48	5.01
2018	90/60	4.70

Macy's Inc. (M)

	High/Low Price	EPS
2012	42/32	2.88
2013	54/26	3.46
2014	66/50	4.01
2015	73/34	4.25
2016	45/29	3.77
2017	36/17	3.11
2018	41/22	4.91

Nordstrom (JWN)

	High/Low Price	EPS
2012	54/43	3.24
2013	59/48	3.56
2014	75/51	3.78
2015	77/49	3.76
2016	62/35	3.31
2017	50/37	3.24
2018	67/43	2.95

J. C. Penney Co Inc. (JCP)

	High/Low Price	EPS
2012	43/15	0.94
2013	23/6	-3.49

2014	11/4	-5.73
2015	10/6	-2.55
2016	11/6	-1.03
2017	8/2	0.08
2018	4/0	0.16

Best Buy (BBY)

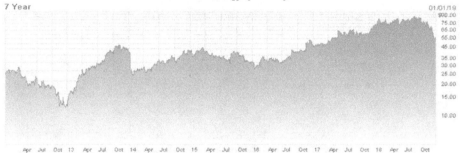

	High/Low Price	EPS
2012	27/11	3.61
2013	44/11	2.55
2014	41/22	2.07
2015	42/28	2.60
2016	49/25	2.78
2017	68/41	3.51
2018	84/47	4.42

Apple

There have been plenty of reasons to buy Apple stock over the years. If you've been investing long enough, you may remember when the idea of buying Apple stock was deemed risky and even speculative before Steve Jobs returned as CEO in 1997. Since the advent of the iPod four years later, the company and stock have been on quite a winning streak.

I know when I decided to buy Apple stock in 2009, two things triggered the decision.

Reason number one was the launch of the iPhone, which led to consumers camping in front of Apple stores to buy it. There was serious buzz around the launch (and a line out the door).

I had used a Blackberry for a couple years with my job and *loved* the device. I knew how much I loved my iPod as well, and the idea of blending the two seemed perfect. In my mind this would be a surefire hit product. You see, Apple didn't really invent the smartphone, they just made a better one, and made more money than anyone else on each phone they sold.

I didn't buy one. I just wanted one. I decided I didn't want to spend the money. The data plans and the phones were expensive, and I had a young family on a budget.

Reason number two was my 22-year-old younger brother. He was fresh from college graduation and struggling to start his career in a terrible job market. He was working part-time cleaning carpets for his future father-in-law's carpet cleaning business. He bought an iPhone.

When my semi-employed little brother bought the new iPhone, I bought Apple stock. (Fast forward, my brother is a now successful investment professional).

Apple Inc. (AAPL)

	High/Low Price	**EPS**
2012	100/57	6.31
2013	82/55	5.68
2014	119/70	6.45
2015	134/92	9.22
2016	118/89	8.31
2017	177/114	9.21
2018	233/146	11.91

Here's the AAPL dividend history since 2015. Notice that the dividend has gone up since then. In February of 2015, the quarterly dividend was $0.47 per share. By 2018, that quarterly dividend had increased to $0.73 per share.

Date Paid	**Dividend**
Feb 5, 2015	0.47
May 7, 2015	0.52
Aug 6, 2015	0.52
Nov 5, 2015	0.52
Feb 4, 2016	0.52
May 5, 2016	0.57
Aug 4, 2016	0.57
Nov 3, 2016	0.57
Feb 9, 2017	0.57
May 11, 2017	0.63
Aug 10, 2017	0.63
Nov 10, 2017	0.63
Feb 9, 2018	0.63
May 11, 2018	0.73

Aug 10, 2018	0.73	
Nov 8, 2018	0.73	

BlackBerry Limited (BB)

	High/Low Price	EPS
2012	17/6	4.20
2013	18/5	-0.61
2014	12/7	-1.35
2015	12/5	-0.09
2016	9/6	-0.24
2017	12/6	0.06
2018	14/6	0.14

Netflix

Netflix has been particularly interesting to follow as a stock and as a company. It's a good example of keeping an eye on trends and gauging if companies you're watching can change with those trends or go down in flames.

The company was able to make the pivot from hard-copy CD rentals to digital streaming entertainment. When the company was formed, the "runner-up" name for the company was DVDbymail.com. What's in a name? Well, I wonder if that transition would have been as successful if it involved a name change too.

Who remembers Blockbuster Video? Anybody want to invest in DVD kiosk company Redbox?

Blockbuster declared bankruptcy in 2010 (wiping out all equity holders) and closed most of its stores in 2013 and 2014. As of the end of 2018, there was one Blockbuster store left in Bend, Oregon.

Certainly, any stock buyers of Redbox parent company Coinstar (later renamed Outerwall) instead of Netflix would rather not remember that decision. Redbox still exists as a part of public company Apollo Global Management, which acquired Outerwall for $900 million in 2016. As of early 2019, Netflix was worth $140 billion.

Netflix was able to navigate the transition in consumer tastes toward streaming and toward original content and not only survive but thrive.

It hasn't necessarily been a smooth ride for investors. After consistently growing subscribers and adding digital streaming in 2007, the company announced in September 2011 it would split into separate services: Netflix would keep streaming and "Qwickster" would become the DVD rental company. Along with the change, the previous $10 a month plan covering both DVD and streaming services would be split into two plans, each costing $8. The company misjudged the way customers would react, lost subscribers, and the stock price was cut in half.

Just to prove that even the experts aren't always experts, at the time of Netflix's separation into business units for DVD and streaming businesses, an analyst was quoted on reuters.com[1] saying: "There's still a lot of backlash from the price increase before. At this point, consumers are still looking for a less expensive alternative such as Coinstar Inc.'s Redbox kiosk." At the time, the analyst rated Netflix shares "neutral" and put a "buy" rating on Coinstar.

Netflix listened to its customers, quickly dropped the "two plan" idea, and regained favor from them and from investors.

Eventually, three things happened:

- People stopped watching DVDs as Wi-Fi-connected TVs and mobile devices became mainstream.
- People began to "cut the cord" and cancel their cable along with subscribing to Netflix and other services.

> Amazon's streaming service was free to Prime subscribers and acted as a complement rather than a competitor to Netflix.
> - Netflix would invest in compelling content and win loyal subscribers who could only see those shows on Netflix.

All of this showed up in earnings over time. In 2011, earnings were $0.59 per share. In 2012, they were $0.04. Earnings wouldn't reach the 2011 level again until 2017, but the stock price had surpassed the 2011 peak by the fourth quarter of 2013. The market is always *looking ahead* six to 18 months at a minimum. It certainly got this one right. Earnings exploded higher in 2017 and 2018.

Netflix Inc. (NFLX)

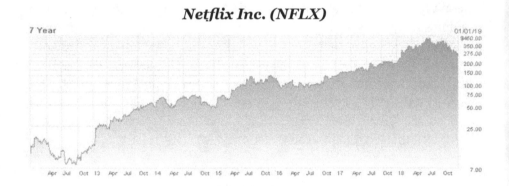

	High/Low Price	EPS
2011	43/8	0.59
2012	19/7	0.04
2013	55/12	0.30
2014	69/42	0.53
2015	133/45	0.31
2016	129/79	0.43
2017	204/123	1.25
2018	423/191	2.68

Google (Alphabet)

Most people—OK, *everyone*—knows Google, but in a 2015 restructuring, Alphabet became the parent, publicly-traded company. Here, I'll talk in terms of Google, because that business is what really drives the stock price.

Google didn't always have such a dominant position in search. I remember using several different engines and learned about Google from an investment website around 2002. I read an article that said (at the time privately-owned) Google's search engine was so much better than anyone else's, that the term Google would become a verb. I wish I had saved that article, because it proved right, and now I have no clue who to thank for the insight.

The technology behind what makes Google better is well beyond my brain. I just know that I started Googling things and did substantially less Yahooing things or Asking Jeeves or whatever else I was doing prior to Google.

In 1999, early internet portal Excite.com CEO George Bell turned down a chance to buy Google from the founders for $1 million, and then also declined a counter-offer of $750,000. Oops.

As of this writing, Google has a market cap of over $700 billion. Excite. com was eventually acquired in 2004 by ask.com for an undisclosed amount. Ask.com was eventually taken private for $1.8 billion. I'm not sure what the asset is worth at this point, but it isn't even close to Google's gargantuan market cap.

Nerd Word Alert

Private Equity Firm: Investment banking companies that specialize in buying assets in distress and taking them private. Typically, they will look to restructure companies or fix problems, then resell all or parts of the businesses for a higher price.

Whether Google had the better technology or not, they certainly had the traffic by the time they went public in 2004. It came to market with an IPO share price of $85 and a market cap of $23 billion.

With the adoption of the mobile internet, they have seen their profits grow at an incredible rate the last several years. In 2012, they made $17.21 per share. In 2017 they made $35.90 per share and in 2018 earnings increased to $45.18 per share.

Alphabet Inc. (GOOGL)

	High/Low Price	EPS
2011	323/236	18.03
2012	387/278	17.21
2013	560/347	19.42
2014	614/497	19.82
2015	798/490	24.34
2016	839/672	27.85
2017	1086/789	35.90
2018	1291/977	45.18

Note

1) "Netflix splits DVD and streaming services"; September 19, 2011; Lisa Richwine, Yinka Adegoke; Reuters; https://www.reuters.com/article/us-netflix/netflix-splits-dvd-and-streaming-services-idUS-TRE78I23B20110919?sp=true

18 | Show & Tell: A Little Wisdom From Kids

This book summarizes many of the stories and concepts I've taught financial professionals over my career. I used these same concepts to teach my kids, but then they did a funny thing. They taught me, and said things I found myself quoting at work.

One of my motivations for writing this book has been observing how well kids understand and enjoy this investing game. They are smart at a young age and will surprise you with what they pick up.

Apple night

When Max was six (his younger siblings were four and five), he gave us the zinger in the picture below from my personal Facebook page. (This was before they had even saved up enough money in the $500 challenge to be able to afford any stock.) In hindsight, think I should have given him more credit at the time for knowing exactly what he was saying.

7 years ago

Joseph John Wenrich
December 28, 2011 at 4:09 PM · 🏠

I have the kids plus my niece and nephew tonight - sell-out that I am, we break out the ipods and ipads - my six year old (max) says "its an apple night - no wonder the stock is $400!" - Of course he has no clue what that means, but its still cool, right???

👍 Travis Pepperd and 7 others   4 Comments

↪ Share

Don't sell, buy more

More recently, Max was in his eighth-grade art class and overheard classmates discussing a stock market game from their math class. They were discussing their holdings, and he heard one of them say, "We should sell it while it's low, before it gets any lower."

Max, always the one to bluntly give unsolicited advice, tells them, "You're doing it wrong. You want to buy them low and sell them high."

"What do you mean?" they replied.

"If it's lower, it will eventually go up as long as it's something good and not going out of business. If you sell it low, you won't make any money. You should probably try to buy more."

I think he gets it!

Pop Tarts

Here's another gem I heard from a financial advisor's son one morning:

> *"Dad, who makes Pop-Tarts? These are great and I bet they make a lot of money!"*

The duck company

The power of a strong brand can help create interest in a company's stock too. This conversation with my daughter made that clear:

> *Annabel: "Dad, can I buy stock of the company with the duck?"*
>
> *Me: "AFLAC? Do you know what they do?"*
>
> *Annabel: "Something about insurance. They pay you when you can't work."*

Early retirement

On another evening, I was showing the kids their accounts. They had owned their stocks for about a year. I showed them they had more cash in the account than the last time they looked, even though they had not made any deposits. We looked at the account activity history and found that they were receiving dividends. And not only were they receiving dividends, but the dividends had increased.

Max looked at it, processed for a moment, tilted his head, and proceeded to blow my mind.

"I need to just keep buying shares of companies that pay dividends now while I'm young. That way, when I'm old like you, the shares can pay my income and I won't have to work so hard."

He speaks the truth. He should write a book!

Glossary

Active Fund

Mutual fund or ETF designed to beat the return of a particular market or index.

Acquisition

When one company buys another. It can also be called a "takeover."

Appraisal

The process for estimating how much an asset is worth in the market.

Asset

Something of value that can be sold.

Asset Class

A group of assets with similar characteristics. For example, cash or equities.

Balance Sheet

A report or "financial statement" showing a company's equity, assets, and liabilities.

Bankruptcy

A federal court procedure that helps businesses settle debts and repay creditors, protecting them from creditors through the process. Bankruptcies can have either reorganization or liquidation as the objective.

Behavioral Finance

The psychology of economic decision making.

Blue Chips

Well-known, well-established, larger companies that have established track records.

Bond

A type of *loan* to an entity that can be bought or sold by investors. Stronger companies pay lower rates, weaker companies pay higher rates. A few types of bonds:

- U.S. Treasury Bonds issued by the U.S. government. These are considered the safest bonds in the world.
- Foreign Government Bonds issued by other countries to finance government operations.
- U.S. Municipal Bonds issued by city, state, and local governments.
- U.S. Corporate Bonds issued by U.S.-based corporations.

Bulls and Bears

If you think a stock will go up in price, you are a "Bull" or "Bullish." If you think a stock will go down in price, you are a "Bear" or "Bearish."

Capital Appreciation

The difference between what you paid for a stock and the unrealized or realized capital gain (loss).

Cash

An investment that you can access for spending relatively quickly with almost no risk of loss.

Certificate of Deposit (CD)

A cash investment offering a slightly higher rate than savings accounts but requiring you to keep it in the account for a specified length of time.

Compound Interest

Earning interest on interest, over time.

Convertible Bond

A bond with a provision that lets you convert it to equity (stock shares) in the bond issuer. The share amount is predetermined by the issuer and available periodically during the life of the bond.

Coupon

The interest payment on a bond. The term originated when bonds were issued in paper form and you would tear off a "coupon" from the bond twice a year and trade it in for cash.

Credit Risk

The risk that you don't get paid back.

Current Yield

The annual yield earned on a bond at the current market price.

Discount

Bonds trading lower than their par value.

Dividend

A portion of company earnings paid in cash to investors.

$$Cash\ payout \div Total\ shares = Dividend$$

Dividend Yield

You may see this term on a quote screen, noted as a percentage of the current price.

$$Dividend\ per\ share \div Share\ price = Dividend\ yield$$

Dollar-cost Averaging

A strategy of investing an equal dollar amount on a schedule over time so you are naturally purchasing more shares when markets are low and fewer shares when markets are high.

Earnings Projections

Estimates for future earnings per share from analysts that follow a company.

Equity

The ownership interest in a business.

Equity = Assets - Liabilities

Exchange Traded Fund (ETF)

Similar to a mutual fund, but shares can be traded throughout the day.

Forward-looking Statements

The nerdiest way possible to say "predicting the future."

Fundamental Analysis

Considering the business prospects and financial health of a company to form an opinion on a stock. The process in this book uses fundamental analysis.

Index

A collection of stocks used to help measure various aspects of the market. Used for specific groups of stocks. For example, you will see indexes for small stocks, medium stocks, dividend stocks, oil stocks, tech stocks, etc.

Initial Public Offering (IPO)

The process of becoming publicly traded.

Interest

A charge to a person or entity as payment for borrowing money. For investors, this is a source of income when you deposit or loan your money. The amount is usually specified as an annual percentage rate.

Interest Rate Risk

The risk that interest rate changes cause your investments to change in price.

Liabilities

Debts against an individual or company.

Liquidity

A measure of how quickly you can turn invested money into cash to pay for something. The more liquid an investment, the more quickly it can be turned into cash without losses or penalties.

Market Capitalization (market cap)

The total value of a company. Calculated by multiplying the total shares by the share price.

$$MC = (share\ price) \times (total\ shares)$$

Maturity

The date the company (or entity) is obligated to pay an invested or loan amount back to investors.

Monetizing

Turning business metrics like site traffic, users or "eyeballs" into revenue.

Multiple

The number of years of earnings (or sales or another metric) it requires to buy a business.

Multiple Expansion (Contraction)

The PE ratio (multiple) decreasing or increasing.

Mutual Fund

A way to invest in many stocks and/or bonds at once. Your investment is pooled with other investors, and the management company purchases the shares on your behalf. One share of a fund may represent dozens to hundreds of investments inside it. Shares only trade once a day, at the close of the market.

Out-years

What EPS and PE look like based on expectations for a few years from now, not just next year and last year.

Par

Usually $1,000 per bond. The amount the bond issuer must pay back to a bond investor. "At par" means at $1,000.

Passive Fund

Mutual fund or ETF designed to match the return of a particular market or index.

PE Ratio

Price per share ÷ Earnings per share, aka the multiple. It is a ratio used to compare values of different companies compared to earnings.

Premium

Bonds trading higher than their par value.

Primary Market

Investors dealing directly with the company issuing bonds or stocks.

Private Equity Firm

Investment banking companies that specialize in buying assets in distress and taking them private. Typically, they will look to restructure companies or fix problems, then resell all or parts of the businesses for a higher price.

Privately Owned

Mostly smaller, "private" businesses owned by one person or a small number of people. With private ownership shares, there is no formal exchange, so it may take days, months or years to find a buyer or seller.

Publicly Traded

Getting investment money by going through the IPO process to offer shares in the business on a public exchange, like the Nasdaq Stock Market or New York Stock Exchange. The private owners offer some of their shares for public sale in this process.

Range

The high and low price for a time frame.

Rate of Return

The amount of money earned on an investment expressed as a percentage of the original investment. $100 invested that earns $10 made a rate of return of: $10 ÷ $100 = 0.10 = 10%

Real Estate

Land and buildings.

Realized Capital Gain (Loss)

The difference between the price you buy and sell. If you buy for $10 and sell for $15, you had a realized capital gain of $5. If you buy for $10 and sell for $8, you have a realized capital loss of $2.

Retained Earnings

The portion of earnings not paid out as dividends.

Revenue

Another word for sales.

S&P 500 Index

Represents 500 U.S. stocks with market caps above around $5 billion selected by a committee at the company Standard & Poor's. It's *not* the 500 largest companies, it's the 500 chosen by Standard & Poor's.

Secondary Market

A third-party market for the buying and selling of company stocks and bonds between investors.

Security

Another name for a stock or bond or similar contract that pledges an interest in a business.

Share

A unit of ownership for a company. Think of as your "share of the company."

Stock

Shares of ownership in a company that can be bought or sold by investors.

Stock (Ticker) Symbol

An abbreviation used to identify shares of a particular company traded on a stock market.

Technical Analysis

The science of charting stocks.

Term

The amount of time until a bond or loan must be paid back. A 20-year term bond will be paid back in 20 years.

Time Horizon

The length of time until you are expecting to need the money you are investing.

Total Return

The entire amount of money you make on an investment. For a stock, you earn cash dividends, as well as your capital appreciation or depreciation.

Total Yield

Your return as a percentage. Divide total return by the original investment amount.

Unrealized Capital Gain (Loss)

For an asset you have not sold yet, the difference between the price you bought it for and the current market price. In other words, what would your realized gain or loss would be if you sold it right now.

Volatility

Refers to how much a stock price moves up and down.

Volume

Represents the number of shares that traded ownership that day. The volume bars along the bottom of a stock chart usually look like rectangles lined up in a row.

Appendix

A. Quick and Simple Financial Planning Checklist

- Financial Statement
    - What are your assets? What are your debts? The difference is your net worth.
- Income Statement
    - How much income do you bring in each month/year? How much goes out? The difference is your excess cash flow that you can incorporate into your plan to achieve your goals. You may find it helpful to build a budget to keep yourself disciplined about your spending.
- Cash Reserves
    - The first goal should be a cash reserve. Begin to save regularly and systematically (every paycheck, preferably before you pay your regular bills) into a savings account separate from your primary checking account. Try to get three to six months of expenses saved. This will prevent you from having to sell equities or use debt when unexpected expenses occur.
- Protection Planning
    - The "other first goal" should be protection planning.
        - Life Insurance – If you have loved ones (e.g., spouse, children, parent) who would suffer financial hardship without you, you need life insurance. What would you or they want to see happen if you were to die tomorrow? What goals would you still want to fund? Don't overlook the stay-at-

home spouse. They may not make an income, but ask yourself: How would life change without him or her?

- Disability Insurance – If you were to get sick or hurt and unable to work, how do you pay the bills? Your ability to earn an income is an asset that you should protect. What's your annual income? If you had a machine in your shed that cranked out that much money each year, would you buy insurance on it?

- Long-term Care – Care for when/ if you cannot take care of yourself. While nursing home care comes to mind, many people purchase long-term care to avoid nursing homes. If you have protection, you may be able to afford to stay in your home.

- A note on insurability: Most insurance coverages require you to undergo a medical exam or interview to determine if you are insurable. If you've had health problems, it may be more expensive or even impossible to obtain coverage. For this reason, I recommend purchasing insurance as soon as you can afford it, even if you don't need it until later. You never know when you will become uninsurable.

- Each of these insurance types can get complicated. I recommend you work with a financial planner to help determine what's right for you. Get multiple opinions for your protection needs. There are varying ways to cover these needs. Make sure you are comfortable and understand what you're buying. ASK LOTS OF QUESTIONS.

- Goal Planning

- What are your goals? – Retirement? College savings? Open a business? Buy a house?
- "Needs Before Greeds" – Your first two goals should be Cash Reserves and Protection Planning
- Define your goals –How much would they cost in today's dollars? When do you want to achieve them?
- Prioritize your goals – If you have more goals than money, which goal will you give up, or delay, to achieve another goal?
- Having defined your goals in Step 1, begin to calculate how much it will cost to achieve your goals. Calculate how much you would need to save to achieve your goal at various rates of return.
- What do you have going towards those goals already? Calculate any current savings or investments into your plan. Make sure you take advantage of any retirement and protection benefits available to you from your employer. If you work for a company that provides a retirement plan, take advantage of any employer matching contributions.
- Taxes
  - Do annual tax planning to take advantage of possible deductions.
  - When saving or investing, consider using tax-preferred investment vehicles if appropriate (401(k), IRA, Roth IRA, 529 Plan, etc.). Consider how monies will be taxed both at the time of investment and when you take the money out of the account. Keep in mind, whenever you use a tax-preferred vehicle, you are giving up a level of flexibility. Make sure you understand the rules.
- Estate and End of Life Planning

- Guardianship for minor children – If you don't have a written plan, who will decide who takes care of your children if something happens to you?
- Who do you want making financial decisions if you cannot?
- Who do you want making health care decisions if you cannot?
- How do you feel about life support or other treatments or conditions?
- How do you want your assets distributed?
- Should you consider advanced planning techniques to avoid death and estate taxes?

B. Excel Commands from Chapter 6

For those unfamiliar with Excel, here's a crash course on basic calculations.

Entering the = sign into a cell lets Excel know you want to do a calculation or reference another cell.

> Example: To reference another cell (cell A1), enter "= A1" into another cell. That cell will display the same thing that is displayed in A1. Entering "= A1 + A2" will give you the sum of A1 and A2. This works for addition and subtraction. Use * for multiplication and / for division.

In the following image, you'll see the calculation for 1% interest in the "formula" window, referencing cell B2 as the beginning value multiplied by .01.

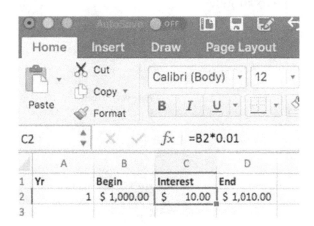

In the following image, you will see adding B2 and C2 for our ending value.

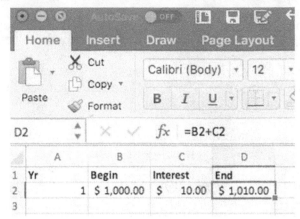

Below are the formulas for year two. Continue this pattern for as many years as you'd like to show.

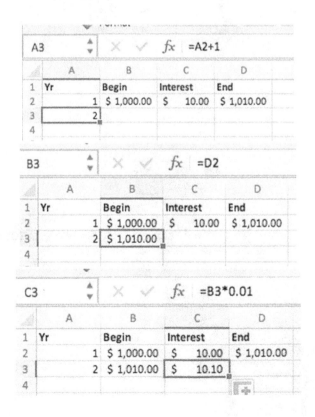

D2		✕ ✓	*fx* =B2+C2	
	A	B	C	D
1	Yr	Begin	Interest	End
2	1	$ 1,000.00	$ 10.00	$ 1,010.00
3	2	$ 1,010.00	$ 10.10	$ 1,020.10
4				

By using "copy and paste" you can fill in other cells quickly without having to type them manually. You can also drag the small square in the bottom right corner of a highlighted cell to fill or "paste" the calculation to other cells.

To show the calculations including monthly additions, simply add a column and add it to the ending total each period.

Thanks to these sites

For the Warren Buffett quotes:

- https://www.suredividend.com/warren-buffett-quotes/
- https://www.benzinga.com/general/education/15/02/5249256/wisdom-of-warren-buffett-keep-it-simple-do-what-works

For EPS and stock price info:

- investors.com
- Nasdaq.com
- Yahoo Finance
- ycharts.com
- cnbc.com
- Google Finance